GREENLAND:
Island at the Top of the World

GREENLAND:
Island at the Top of the World

Madelyn Klein Anderson

Illustrated with photographs and maps

Dodd, Mead & Company   New York

reenland showing the Greenland ice sheet.

1   2   3   4   5   6   7   8   9   10

Library of Congress Cataloging in Publication Data

Anderson, Madelyn Klein.
   Greenland, island at the top of the world.

   Bibliography: p.
   Includes index.
   Summary: Describes the geography and traces the
history of the world's largest island, much of which
lies above the Arctic Circle.
   1. Greenland—History—Juvenile literature.
[1. Greenland—History]   I. Title.
G760.A53   1983   998'.2   82-46003
ISBN 0-396-08139-8

To the memory of Max and Fannie Klein

ACKNOWLEDGMENTS

For their invaluable assistance in preparing this book, I am grateful to the Consulate General of Denmark at New York and Ebba Pedersen of the Danish Information Office for access to photographs; to George Duck of the Explorers Club for his patient pursuit of rare photographs; to William Jaber for his maps; to Karin Mango for reading the manuscript; to the International Ice Patrol, CWO Paul C. Scotti, and the crew of CG 1341, Unites States Coast Guard, for a memorable trip to Greenland; to Dr. Robert Scheina, historian of the United States Coast Guard; and to the editor, Donna Brooks.

Thank you.

Contents

From Greenland's Icy Mountains...

(old missionary hymn)

Grinding, crashing, piling up in angry snarls, the pack ice—six million square miles of frozen Arctic Ocean—moves on the currents, released from winter bondage by the lengthening days and rising temperatures of spring. High above this giant jigsaw puzzle, in a sky turned milky by glare from the ice, the small plane is a speck of color crisscrossing the great arc of horizon.

It is flying a search pattern, looking for icebergs drifting with the pack ice. Below is the Davis Strait, where currents flow south carrying icebergs calved from Greenland's glaciers into the busy shipping lanes of the North Atlantic.

Icebergs are dangerous. Ever since one such moving mountain of ice sank the great *Titanic*, killing over fifteen hundred people, an International Ice Patrol of ships and planes has kept watch over these waters. The patrol cannot stop the bergs—it has tried many times without success—but it can warn ships away from the icebergs' paths.

To the men in the patrol plane, time itself seems to stand still. At three hundred miles an hour the plane barely seems to move through the vast loneliness of sky and ice. Then, suddenly, one of the crew straightens in his seat and raises binoculars to his eyes. He clicks on the mouthpiece of his headset to alert the rest of the men: a berg at two o'clock.

The pilot banks and closes in on the berg so the men can approximate its dimensions and determine its shape for identification purposes. They also want an exact fix on the berg's location and course.

As the iceberg looms larger, the men sense something wrong, something odd and dark about this berg. Perhaps it has an unusual amount of moraine, rocks and dirt embedded from the time it was still part of a great Greenland glacier? No, not rocks, not dirt—but what? The plane dips lower for a closer look, and there, entombed in the ice, is a giant, khaki-camouflaged plane. It is an old four-prop job that the shocked crew identify as a Flying Fortress bomber. The bomber must have crashed onto the Greenland ice cap many years ago, during World War II.

Greenland is almost entirely covered by a sheet of ice that never melts. Each long Greenland winter deposits a fresh layer of snow on the ice sheet, a layer that presses down the snow of previous winters, burying whatever lies there.

At its domed apex, Greenland's centuries-old ice is two miles thick. The pressure of this ice generates heat so intense that the base of the ice sheet liquefies. On this liquid base the ice sheet moves incessantly outward in all directions, propelled by its own weight. Where it reaches the mountains along Greenland's border, the ice sheet fragments into glaciers, rivers of ice that snake through gaps, passes, and valleys until they reach the sea. There the water and tides work away at these tongues of ice, lifting and pushing and melting them until pieces break off with a thunderous roar and tumble into the sea—icebergs.

The view from a patrol plane.

A glacier reaches the sea and breaks off into thousands of icebergs.

[14]

The bomber sighted by the ice patrol crew made this long journey with the ice sheet all the way to the sea. If its iceberg tomb could be tracked to a point from which it could be towed to land, the bomber might yet be retrieved—it had been done before. But darkness and a shortage of fuel force the men back to base. When the patrol returns in the morning there is no trace of the berg. It has moved on, melting, tumbling to maintain its balance, changing to an unrecognizable shape, at some unknown time and in some unknown place to release its ghostly burden into the sea.

Greenland's great ice cap is one of two in the world; the other covers Antarctica. Scientists think of these ice sheets as deserts. Precipitation is less than ten inches a year—no more snowfall than there is rain in the Sahara. The snow is dry and sandlike, and just as winds blow the Sahara's sand into great dust storms, the winds over Greenland's ice sheet blow its snow into terrible storms. These snow deserts differ from sand deserts in one important way, however: there are no oases, although in summer an occasional pool of water will form from melted snow.

Seen from the air and in sunlight, Greenland's ice cap looks enchanted. It glimmers and glows in crystalline shades of gold and rose. Shadows extend in long, gentle rolls of pale purples, blues, greens, and turquoise. But the ice sheet is no fairyland. The Eskimos considered it the home of evil spirits, and with good reason. Yawning crevasses some two miles long scar its outer perimeters, often hidden beneath thin bridges of snow that give way under the weight of dog, sledge, or man. Summer temperatures are the coldest in the world, and glare from the snow can cause blindness. The winds are brutal, sometimes fatal—even when they suddenly turn into warm föhn winds, they make the ice a quicksand of slush. Only three species of animals are known to live on the inhospitable ice sheet—

*The Arctic ice pack of the coast off Greenland with icebergs
frozen in.*

[16]

Soon this iceberg will be freed from the ice pack and will move with the currents.

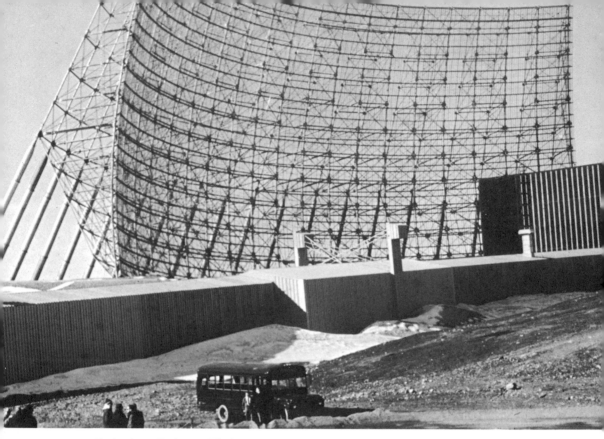

Radar installation at Thule.

foxes, snow buntings, and ravens—although an occasional reindeer or polar bear may accidentally wander onto the ice.

But there are also men living on this ice sheet: scientists doing research and some forty-five technicians at three American radar installations. These technicians live in steel huts mounted on long legs that are periodically raised by hydraulic jack to avoid drifting snow. Food and equipment arrive by airlift. In winter the sun shines for only a few minutes a day. The men are often unable to leave their huts because of the winds, and many have never traveled even one hundred yards from their stations.

What are military outposts doing in such forbidding territory as the Greenland ice cap? Why are the men there? For the same rea-

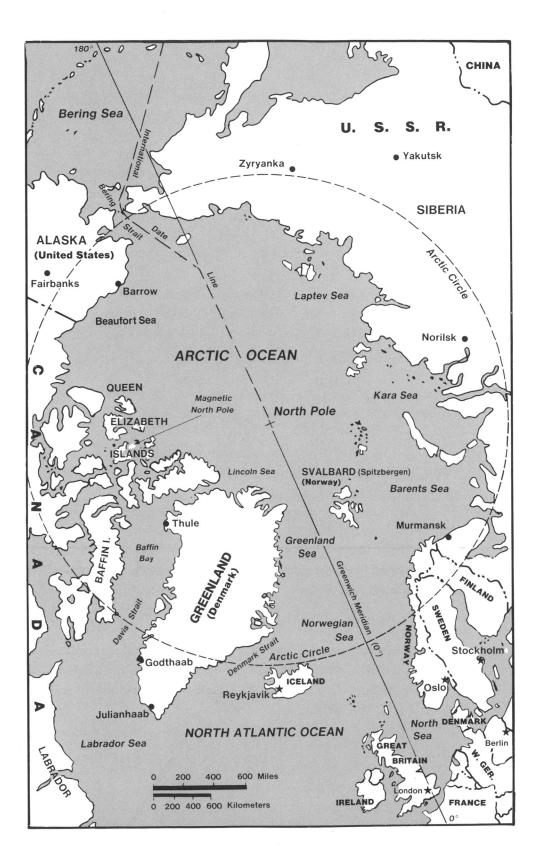

sons that World War II bombers were routed over Greenland and airbases were built there: Greenland is vital to the defense of the European and North American continents.

Greenland is actually part of the North American continent. Once, millions of years ago, Greenland was connected to Canada. Then the continents drifted apart, and the land we call Greenland separated from Canada and became an island, the largest island in the world—844,000 square miles (2,182,000 square kilometers) in size. Greenland's length is about equal to the distance from Scandinavia to North Africa. Much of Greenland lies above the Arctic Circle, and much of it is uninhabitable.

Greenland's population of some fifty thousand people—all of whom could fit comfortably into one pro football stadium in the United States—live only along the edges of the country, because the ice sheet and small local ice caps cover seven-eighths of Greenland. And over 90 percent of the population lives on the western coast. The eastern coast is virtually unreachable except by air. Crossing the ice sheet from west to east is impossible for all but the most intrepid mountain climbers and adventurers. Reaching the east coast by ship is almost as hazardous, because a polar current flows south along the entire east coast and around Cape Farewell at the southern tip of the island, carrying immense floes of pack ice that create an almost impenetrable barrier.

What makes such a forbidding land so important to military strategy? A glance at the map on page 19 will demonstrate: Greenland lies at the top of the world.

Traveling a great circle route over the North Pole shortens the air distance between many major cities. Fly over the top of Greenland and you are in the Soviet Union. The Pacific Ocean and the northwestern United States are closer to the top of Greenland than is New York City, even though Greenland is east of the United States.

During World War II, bombers on their way to war zones in Eu-

Searching for icebergs.

rope refueled on airstrips the United States built in Greenland. Greenland was also vital for weather forecasting. Greenland's ice sheet is known as Europe's weather factory. Prevailing winds make Greenland's weather on Monday the weather in northern Europe on Tuesday, and knowing the weather ahead of time is a distinct advantage in ordering bombing strikes or other military missions.

Today, of course, we have satellites to show us the weather around the world, and computers to do long-range forecasting. But Greenland's location still makes it strategic to North American defense. Those three huts on the ice sheet, along with two airbases on the west coast of Greenland, are part of the United States's Distant Early Warning system, the DEW line, which monitors ballistic missile activity in the northern half of the world.

Geography always plays a role in history, in what happens to a country and its people, and nowhere more strongly than in Greenland. Greenland's history is not really one of development, growth or expansion, or even of wars like most other countries. Rather, it is the story of the use of the country's location: by whalers hunting their prey; by explorers searching for a short route to the riches of the Orient or trying to reach the North Pole; by scientists seeking to understand the nature of Arctic ice and weather; by adventurers testing their courage against the ice; by military men planning their campaigns; and by Norwegians, Danish, Dutch, British, French, Germans, Swiss, Americans ... and, at the very beginning, by Vikings and Skraelings.

Vikings and Skraelings

Greenland is a land of ice and rock, of gray fog and blinding white snow. It is a land of contrasts, of long winter blackness and never-setting summer sunshine, of great beauty and utter desolation. Greenland is many colors—but Greenland is not green, except for a few brief weeks in summer in places where the ice sheet does not reach. Then the dwarf junipers are renewed, the willows weep along the ground, and yellow poppies, gray-green grasses, pink and ivory ranunculus, and birches just a few inches high make the land gay under the never-setting sun.

At one time, millions of years before it was named, Greenland was always green and had an almost tropical climate. Scientists have found fossils of foliage from tropical trees like the fig and the magnolia. But then the Ice Age covered much of the northern world, and when the ice finally retreated as the world warmed, Greenland's ice cap remained, and grew, and Greenland's glaciers calved icebergs into its seas.

How then did Greenland get its name?

A Viking seafarer and exiled murderer gave Greenland its name. He was Eric the Red, probably best known to us as the father of Leif Ericson, the Viking who discovered America before Columbus. There are several theories about Eric the Red's choice of names for the country *he* discovered. When Eric arrived there a thousand years ago, about 982 A.D., the land may have been greener than it is today. There was a time, from about 88 A.D. to 1200 A.D., when the world was warmer than it is now. Even now summer makes the land green deep inside the fjords, around lakes, brooks, snow marshes, and the water holes that form at the melting edges of the ice sheet, or where there are hot springs, as near Disko Bay. Southern Greenland, where Eric settled, has more precipitation than the rest of the island, and dwarf trees, shrubs, herbs, mosses, and nearly two hundred and fifty species of flowering plants flourish there. Even in the far north there are some one hundred flowering plant species that bloom for a few summer weeks when the sun shines day and night. In a warmer era these green areas would have been more extensive and lasted longer. It is also possible that Greenland was simply greener than Eric's home, Iceland. And if Iceland, which has no ice, could be called Iceland, why couldn't Greenland be called green?

The Icelandic *Sagas* say that Eric chose the name Greenland because "... people would all the more desire to go there if the land had an attractive name." The *Sagas,* written in the eleventh and twelfth centuries, are one of the world's great bodies of literature. They are based on stories of Norse kings, nobles, explorers, and heroes both legendary and real, which were passed from generation to generation by word of mouth before they were written down. For this reason, there are some who discount the *Sagas* as pure fiction. But this is no more the truth than saying they are completely factual. There are elements of both fact and fiction in the *Sagas.* Scholars are still sorting them out, and archeologists are confirming what they can from their digs. What we know of early Greenland we know from the *Sagas* and from a twelfth century geography, *Speculum Regae,* or *The King's Mirror,* a work of such superb observation and scholarship that it was not amplified until the nineteenth century.

The *Sagas* tell us that Iceland, the first source of Greenland's settlers, had itself originally been settled by the Irish, great sailors as well as missionaries for Christianity, and by a few Scots. Then the Vikings came to Iceland. The Vikings were sea rovers, explorers, and pirates originally from the Norse, or Scandinavian, countries of Norway, Denmark, and Sweden. They plundered and pillaged all the way from Siberia to France. They also settled, sometimes voluntarily and sometimes because they had been exiled from their own homes. Many of the Vikings who went to Iceland were exiled murderers, Eric the Red's father among them. When they decided on Iceland for their new home, they simply took the Irishmen and Scotsmen as slaves, and appropriated the women as second wives.

Surprisingly enough, this unlikely crew set up in Iceland the world's first parliament and a system of "law readers" to keep the law—more or less. And so, when red-headed Eric lost his temper and killed a man, Icelandic law and parliament sent him into exile.

The *Sagas* say that a hundred years before Eric's exile, an Icelandic sailor by the name of Gunnbjorn had told of a land to the west of Iceland, which he had seen on a voyage but had not explored. Eric probably knew Gunnbjorn's story from the storytellers of the time. He might even have seen the land himself before he sailed, for at certain times from certain hills in Iceland, Greenland's ice-bound eastern coast is visible. At any rate, Eric set sail southwestward from Iceland, across sixteen or so miles of water, looking for Gunnbjorn's land. With Eric went between twenty and forty people—his wife, children, his slaves, and freed men and women—as well as ponies, cattle, sheep, goats, dogs, and pigs, along with food and forage for all. This in a boat about eighty feet long, sixteen and a half feet wide, and seven feet deep, with a single sail and no compass.

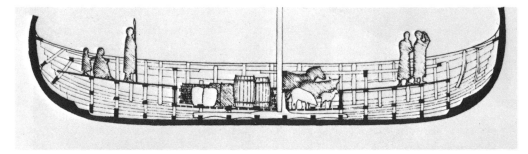

Diagram of the type of boat Eric the Red sailed.

They apparently made land without incident, beaching at what is now the Julienhaab district of southwest Greenland. Eric, who seems to have had a way with names, called this settlement on the western coast the "Eastern Settlement." Why? One theory has it that Eric mistook west for east. But a great Viking seafarer, who could navigate by the sun, moon, and stars, and who explored Greenland's coastline far to the north, could not have made such a mistake. A more likely explanation is that the Vikings of the day did not use directions like "northwest" or "southeast" but simply "west" and "east." In Greenland, the south lies more to the east than does the north, so to Eric the settlement in the southeast was logically the Eastern Settlement. Eric later established a Western Settlement further north (near present-day Godthaab, Greenland's capital).

After three years of exile Eric went back to Iceland to entice more settlers to his green land. Perhaps the name worked after all, or perhaps it was also the promise of good grazing land and fine hunting for seals, reindeer, and musk oxen. Whatever the reasons, Eric left Iceland with about twenty-five boatloads of prospective settlers. Only fourteen, carrying a total of about three hundred and fifty people, seem to have made it to Greenland. The rest were either lost in storms or turned back. Still, three hundred and fifty was a goodly number—only one hundred and two settlers landed at Plymouth Rock in 1620.

The Icelanders seem to have been content with what they found in Greenland, for soon there was a steady stream of immigrants starting farms along the coves, fjords, and bays that indent Greenland's western coast.

The first homes, built of sod and stone, had only one long, narrow room with a stone floor. Fires were laid almost anywhere on the floor. Later, houses were divided into small rooms, possibly for added warmth. The rear wall of the house held the main cooking hearth and was located next to a source of water. Some houses had stone gutters running from the water through the rear wall and into a basin in the middle of the house. Overflow spilled into a narrow channel and out under a side wall. The flow could be shut off by covering the gutter with stones. An on-off water supply was not only a household convenience but also a lifesaving device in the event of an attack. There is some evidence that there were attacks; although these settlers were now farmers, they were still Vikings, and Vikings were easy killers.

For the most part, however, those fierce Vikings were tamed into their roles as farmers and dairymen. Eric had extensive pastures and a barn with stalls for forty cows at his farm, Brattahild, in the Western Settlement. The Vikings established a parliament and law readers modeled after the system they had known in Iceland. And they entered into trade, exporting butter, wool, and furs, and importing lumber, iron, and tools. Trade with Iceland and Norway was brisk, and ships moved frequently and freely between the countries, although a voyage back and forth could take several years.

It was on a return voyage from Norway that Leif Ericson was blown off course and landed somewhere along the coast of North America in what he called Vinland. With him were two priests he was bringing to Greenland at the insistence of King Olaf of Norway, a devout Christian. Even though the Viking men despised Christianity as a religion of the Irish and women, Leif realized he had to keep the Norwegian king happy if trade routes were to be kept open between Greenland and Norway. When Leif finally returned to Greenland with the priests, his mother, Tjoldhild, built a church near Brattahild for those who would practice Christianity with her. Her church was the first in North America. Tjoldhild built well, see-

Ruin of a Viking church.

ing to it that the church was constructed with more rocks than sod. Sod gave warmth, but rocks were permanent, and a church should last. And last it did, for it was standing in Greenland long after the Vikings themselves had disappeared.

Eric's sons and daughter went on more trips to Vinland and then to lands they called Markland and Helleland. The exact locations of these places are the subject of many scholarly arguments. Leif's brother and sister even attempted to colonize Markland, but fierce attacks by people they called "Skraelings," or "howlers," drove them out. No further colonization was attempted, but the Vikings continued to travel to Markland, Helleland, and Vinland for wood and grapes.

The Skraelings showed up in Greenland, too. At least that's what the Viking inhabitants of Greenland called them, apparently because they looked the same as the people they had encountered in Markland. Perhaps they were.

The people the Vikings called Skraelings we know as Eskimos. They were entering the north of Greenland about 1000 A.D., roughly the same time that Eric the Red and his followers were entering the south. The two groups seem to have had no contact for many years. Eric and the Vikings had seen some signs of human occupation—a few stone utensils and remnants of two skin boats that experts today say belonged to a pre-Eskimo culture.

There appear to have been five pre-Eskimo cultures in Greenland, the first entering the country at about 1000 B.C., each one killed off or absorbed by the next. Over thousands of years these peoples migrated from Mongolia, across Siberia, and then across the Bering Strait between Siberia and the North American continent. They probably crossed by a land bridge that arose when the Ice Ages froze the oceans, lowering them as much as three hundred feet. The pre-Eskimos were a late migration, following at least two major migrations of the peoples called "Indians." The earlier migrations had fanned southward, but some of these peoples moved north again to join later migrations of pre-Eskimos. Therefore the Eskimo of today has both Mongolian and American Indian physical characteristics.

Over the centuries, these cultures moved across the high north, following game across the dry, prairie-like land—the high north of Greenland is surprisingly ice-free. The earliest culture had bows and arrows. Later immigrants, a pre-Eskimo culture called Dorset, did not have the bow and arrow, but they did have harpoons with which they hunted whale and seal. The Dorsets also developed the snow house, or igloo, cleverly engineered to shelter them snugly while they were on the hunt. In summer their permanent homes were tents of skins stretched over whalebone frames, and in winter tiny stone and sod huts.

The Dorsets were replaced by another pre-Eskimo culture, the Thule. The great contribution of the Thule culture was the kayak. A lightweight skin boat, swift and silent, it was—and is today—just the right thing for stealing up on seal or whale to make a kill.

The Thules were the last of the pre-Eskimo cultures to arrive in Greenland. The people who came after them, somewhere around 1000 A.D., were those we call Eskimo. The word "Eskimo" was not coined until the 1600s, when a French priest in Canada adapted the word "Esquimaux" from the Algonquian Indian word "Ush-ke-um-wau," which means "raw meat eaters." The Algonquian Indians referred to the peoples of the far north in that way because they ate a tremendous amount of meat, often raw. Explorers in the late 1800s told of Eskimos eating some fifteen pounds of meat per person in half a day.

The Eskimos of Alaska, Canada, and Greenland had their own name for themselves, however: "Inuit" (pronounced In'-you-eet), which means, simply, "the People." Today "Inuit" is the proper way to refer to these peoples, but for clarity in discussing history, the historical name "Eskimo" is used.

No one knows when the Eskimos moving south in Greenland reached the settlements of the Vikings. When they did, they seem to have coexisted peacefully enough, although Eskimo folklore and the Norse *Sagas* tell of a Skraeling attack in the late eleventh century, when the Eskimos killed eighteen Vikings and took two boys as thralls, or slaves.

But for the most part the two cultures seem to have respected one another's rights. The Eastern and Western Settlements both grew and flourished, and by 1125 held some ten thousand inhabitants living in much the same way as Europeans of the time. They had embraced Christianity and had numerous churches, a cathedral, and a bishop, Arnalf, sent to Greenland by the Pope. There were prosperous farmers, hunters, and traders.

Trade was good. Tusks of ivory from the narwhal whale and the walrus commanded great sums, and walrus hides were in demand for making ropes. Furs from Greenland graced the robes of the rich in Europe; its seal and whale blubber lit Europe's lamps. Polar bears were trapped and sold live to courtiers and merchants to give as gifts—and bribes—to kings. Royalty also demanded Greenland falcons, fabled for their hunting abilities. On a less exalted level, Greenland cows provided huge vats of butter for export; Greenland sheep provided the wonderful silky wool typical of sheep in northern climes; and Greenland homespun was considered the finest in the world. Greenland was a prosperous country.

Perhaps this prosperity was beginning to falter around 1260, when the parliament and people of Greenland decided to give up their independence and join their country to the kingdom of Norway. In return, the Greenlanders were to receive trade privileges and also protection from English and Scottish pirates who had been preying on their shipping. The Greenlanders may have thought they were entering into an equal partnership with Norway, but it didn't work out that way. They received neither privileges nor protection.

Piracy flourished, trade did not. The Norwegian government seems to have lost interest in Greenland and to have given up its responsibilities when it sold the right to exclusive trade with Greenland to a private group of Norwegian merchants. Apparently profits did not justify expenses for the merchants, because they neglected Greenland trade until only one or two boats a year made the trip between the two countries. And since a round trip might take as long as five years on account of ice, provisions for the crew took up more space than did goods for trade. Little profit could be made that way.

Strangely enough, the two Greenland settlements also seem to have lost touch with one another. In 1350, a rare visitor from the Western Settlement reported that he found no people at all in the Eastern Settlement, only stray cattle. Norway paid no attention. She was too busy fighting wars and negotiating with Denmark to join into one kingdom.

What little information we have of these times seems to show that the Greenlanders were moving north, where the hunting was better. In the year 1333, three hunters wintered on the island of Kingiktorsuak, about two hundred miles north of Disko Bay, almost halfway up the coast of Greenland. The men built three cairns, tall piles of stones that stood out like beacons. Over the centuries in the Arctic, cairns were widely used to mark gravesites or to leave messages. The Kingiktorsuak cairns left a message on a small slate stone: *Erling Sigvatsson and Bjorne Thordsson and Enridi Oddsson on the Saturday before Gangdag* (April 24) *made these cairns.* So we know the Vikings were still there, and we also know that the church remained active, because records of the time tell of a Greenlander burned at the stake and of a marriage.

The last ship known to have reached Greenland arrived in 1410. Some say that there were no more ships because the only men who knew the route to Greenland were all killed in a drunken brawl in

Fourteenth-century European clothing found in Greenland graveyards, showing that there was contact between Greenland and Europe during this period.

Runic stone found at the cairn erected by Sigvatsson, Tordsson, and Oddsson.

Norway. Had the way to Greenland become so difficult, perhaps because of ice, that only experienced sailors could find it? This seems hard to believe when ships had successfully been navigating the course for four centuries. Some sort of contact must have been made, because a letter from Pope Nicholas V written in the mid-1400s tells of pirates making terrible fire attacks on Greenland.

After this letter there is nothing but silence for the next one hundred years.

This Greenlandic civilization of almost four centuries, this once prosperous country with its cathedral and churches, its parliament and laws, its thriving sea trade and its ships capable of freely crossing the Atlantic long before Columbus—these ten thousand or more Viking people simply disappeared. And to this day, no one knows for sure why or how.

But the Skraelings survived. Did they kill off the Vikings? That was the theory years ago. But why would they, after centuries of peaceful coexistence? Eskimo legends tell of killings, but not of an entire people. The Eskimos did murder for revenge, and blood feuds sometimes lasted for generations and were considered proper: "an eye for an eye." But disagreements were more often settled in a civilized manner: drum dances and song contests in which the opponents ridiculed each other until one of them ran out of things to say

A nineteenth-century cairn marking someone's burial place
(photographed during World War II).

A song and drum contest.

and, humiliated, was declared the loser. Here are lyrics from one song contest in which the Assailant is the former husband, the Adversary the present husband of a Greenlandic woman:

Assailant: Let me split words,
small, sharp words
like wood I split
with an axe.
A song from old times
A breath from my forefathers
A Lethean song for my wife
A song which may sink the longing
overpowering me.
A bold chatterer has taken her away,
has tried to make her less,
a miserable who loves human flesh
a cannibal from time of starvation.

Adversary: Boldness that surprises!
Mock anger and courage!
A libellous ditty
throwing the blame on me!

Fear thou wilt strike into me
while careless I expose myself to be killed.
Hie—thou singest about my wife
who once was thine;
then thou wert not nearly so lovable.

While she was alone
Thou forgotest to praise her in song,
in challenging battle songs.
Now she is mine,
nor shall she visit false lovers,
beautifully singing lovers of women
in strange tents.

Mass murder of the Viking population is more likely to have been carried out by pirates than Eskimos—if murder of an entire civilization was possible.

It seems more probable that peaceful coexistence—intermarriage with the Skraelings—caused the disappearance of the Vikings. Without the goods that the trading ships used to bring, the European-style society of the Vikings may have proved inadequate for survival. Or the food supply may have failed. A period of icy cold, called the Little Ice Age, attacked the northern hemisphere between 1200 and 1600. Farming could have become impossible, as it is impossible today in Greenland. Cattle and sheep may have died. Archeologists have discovered evidence, too, that enormous invasions of caterpillars descended on the Western Settlement in the 1400s, eating crops and grasses used for forage. The Vikings might very well have turned to the Eskimo style of life when their own European habits and customs failed.

In the late 1400s, a few half-hearted attempts were made to reach the Viking colony in Greenland. In 1472 or 1473, the Norwegians sent a mapping expedition to Greenland at the request of the Portuguese, great navigators and explorers. The expedition was carried off course by storms and currents, however, and gave up its mission entirely. It went home without even sighting Greenland's coast. The Catholic Church also made two feeble attempts to mount an expedition to find its congregation, but second thoughts and problems kept the ships at dock.

And so Greenland faded into the long Arctic night. The fate of the Viking colony, hidden by time, distance, and neglect, is one of the great mysteries of history.

3

Whalers, Explorers, and Eskimos

The search that brought Columbus to the American continent also brought Greenland back into world history. Greenland became—almost accidentally—part of the great search for a Northwest Passage, a sea route from the Atlantic to the Pacific oceans. Europeans hoped to find a way for their ships to reach the spice markets of the Orient by sailing west through America. Spices in those days before refrigeration were worth more than gold: they preserved food and covered the taste of spoiled meat. The overland journey to the spice markets were bedeviled by thieves, however, and the sea journey via the Mediterranean and Red seas and the Indian Ocean was menaced by pirates.

For hundreds of years men searched for a Northwest Passage, exploring every bay and inlet in the waters between Greenland and Canada. While they were at it, the early explorers also searched for the lost Viking colonies of Greenland. They didn't find anyone they considered to be of European descent—they seem to have thought that the Vikings would still be dressed in European clothes and living in towns. Later explorers were more sophisticated and sought signs of the Vikings in physical characteristics like blue eyes and light hair among the Eskimos. But by then there had been so many contacts with whalers and explorers, and so many children of mixed European and Eskimo parentage, that it was impossible to tell whether any were Viking descendants.

The explorers looking for the Northwest Passage to the Indies were more interested in exploration than in history and lost colonies, anyway. One of the first, Martin Frobisher, was particularly interested in gold. Frobisher sailed north from England in 1576 and 1577, and landed in Greenland in 1578, the first European to arrive there in almost two centuries. Frobisher was not particularly successful in the Arctic, however. He thought Greenland was a different island altogether—Friesland—and so mapped Greenland far to the north of where it actually lies. This caused later mariners no end of grief as they piled up in the ice and fog off southern Greenland— where Greenland wasn't supposed to be. Frobisher also thought he had reached China when he had actually landed in Canada, but of course Columbus thought he had reached India, so perhaps this error on Frobisher's part is understandable—except Frobisher made his voyages eighty years after Columbus. Frobisher brought back an Eskimo to England to prove he had found the Chinese, and a lot of worthless rocks to prove he had found gold. Eric the Red had done far better than that seven hundred years earlier, without the aid of a compass such as Frobisher had. Perhaps it is poetic justice that an angry Eskimo, who had traded for one of the Englishmen's muskets, used it to shoot Frobisher in the buttocks. Fortunately for Frobisher, the wound proved more embarrassing than dangerous, and he went on to more successful exploits under Sir Francis Drake in the West Indies and against the Spanish Armada.

John Davis, another Englishman, visited Greenland three times. In 1587, Davis explored the long body of water between Canada and Greenland that now bears his name, the Davis Strait. Davis gave the name "Frobisher Strait" to a body of water that he thought crossed southern Greenland, another error in charting the geography of Greenland that would confuse mariners and explorers for centuries. To his credit, Davis knew at least that he was not in China and that the Eskimos were not the Chinese. And he knew how to behave as a guest in someone else's country. The Davis expeditions got along famously with the Eskimos. The ship's four-piece orchestra played for dancing, a favorite pastime of the Eskimos. Some of the dances they learned from Davis's men are still danced by Greenlanders today. Another Eskimo delight, a game of ball, cemented the relationship between the two groups. The sailors traded their guns, knives, combs, needles, and pots for kayaks and Eskimo clothing— Davis was particularly impressed with the quality and artistry of the clothing made of seal and bird skins—and everyone was content.

While most explorers were seeking a Northwest Passage to the Indies, the possibility of a Northeast Passage also brought explorers to the far north. They reasoned that a passage through Greenland and other islands in the Arctic and Siberia would eventually bring them to the Pacific Ocean. William Barents, a Dutch navigator, was one of the explorers interested in finding a Northeast Passage. He reached what is now Spitsbergen and, possibly because it was joined by ice to Greenland and seemed to be part of it, charted Spitsbergen as part of Greenland. It was another error that would not be corrected for hundreds of years in geography and history books. Most of Barents's charts were so accurate, however, that he is considered one of the most important of the early Arctic explorers. The data he collected on climate, weather, and ice conditions in the Arctic are consulted even today.

Another great early explorer of the Arctic was Henry Hudson, who sailed for the Dutch and then for the English. Like Barents, he sought a Northeast Passage. But he eventually abandoned that search and sailed to the mainland of North America, discovering most of its east coast bays before sailing again to Greenland to try for the Northwest Passage. In 1610, he discovered the vast strait and bay in Canada that now bear his name: Hudson Strait and Hudson Bay. A great sailor, Hudson almost reached the North Pole. He was only 575 nautical miles away when his ship became trapped in ice. He and his crew were forced to wait for the spring thaw. But when spring came and the ship finally broke free, mutiny erupted at Hudson's announcement that they would continue exploring rather than go home. The mutineers set Hudson, his son, and loyal members of the crew adrift in a small boat with neither food nor water. They were never heard from again.

Hudson's mutinous crew, minus four members killed in an encounter with Eskimos, returned to England. Mutiny was usually harshly dealt with, but these mutineers went unpunished because they were able to be useful. They had experience in the Arctic and could guide another explorer, Sir William Baffin, and another ship, the *Discovery,* on yet another search for the Northwest Passage. In 1615–1616, the mutineers and Sir William discovered Baffin Bay, Baffin Land, Smith Sound, and Lancaster Sound. But Baffin also reported that there was no Northwest Passage, and the rush of explorers to the waters around Greenland slowed down for a time.

Other expeditions were heading to Greenland, however. In 1605, a Danish-Norwegian expedition was sent to Greenland to reopen that colony to trade. It found the Eskimos eager for items of iron and steel, a natural enough desire in a country where the only iron came from seldom found pieces of meteorite. Trading was accomplished by Eskimos pointing to what they wanted and then laying out the skins, blubber, and tusks they were willing to offer in exchange. Articles were added or subtracted on both sides until agreement was reached.

The Danish-Norwegian trading expedition actually did much of its trading in Spitsbergen, assuming they were in Greenland. But their impact was strongly felt, for they kidnapped three Eskimos to bring back to Denmark and Norway for exhibition like exotic zoo animals, and as proof of the expedition's landfall. The three Eskimos seem to have enjoyed their captivity—their European clothing, swords, plumes, and all the fuss made over them. They were sent home the following year, but two died on the way, and history does not record the fate of the third.

Dozens more Eskimos were taken from their homes by various expeditions. Although they were treated well, what were these people to make of their plight? Torn from their families, ignorant of European customs and foods, not knowing when, if ever, they would return to their native land, some committed suicide. Some, it is said, died of homesickness, and still others died of European sicknesses like smallpox and influenza, to which they had little or no immunity. In Greenland, the names of the kidnapped who did not return were remembered for many years in stories handed down from generation to generation.

Not all the Eskimos who went to Norway and Denmark had to be kidnapped. Some volunteered to go and were royally received. One, Poek, became a celebrity among his people when he returned with valuable gifts and stories of abundance—of various kinds. Poek told, for instance, of "many houses where the householder does nothing but sell water which makes you quite mad. There they drink and yell and scream and fight and are without reason." Being "without reason" was an unthinkable state for the Eskimos, but Poek forgot his own reason when he went back to Denmark a second time with

A painting of Poek (left) and Quiperoq. The painting hangs in the National Museum, Copenhagen, Denmark.

[44]

his wife, and he turned to the "maddening water." Poek and his wife never returned to Greenland—they died of smallpox in Denmark.

Another wave of Europeans descended upon Greenland in the seventeenth century. Again, they were there because of Greenland's geography. These Europeans were whalers searching for the Greenland, or right, whale, the humpback whale, the white and blue whales, the great gray whale, and the narwhal. The narwhal is one

Full-grown narwhal (male). The small eye is pointed out.

of the family of toothed whales. Its tooth, a magnificent long twisted tusk of ivory, is the reason some people believe that the narwhal is the unicorn of folklore and mythology. The narwhal's tusk was greatly prized by whalers because they could get a lot of money for it. Powdered "unicorn's horn" was—and is—considered magical by some cultures. The ivory tusks of the walrus were also valuable. But it was the baleen of the toothless whales that made the whalers rich. Baleen, also called whalebone, is a flexible, comblike substance, which hangs by the hundreds from the upper jaw of the toothless whales and acts as a strainer for plankton, their food supply. Baleen was ideal for shoring up the corsets and umbrellas of Europe, and for making chair and carriage springs. Both toothed and toothless whales also supplied blubber, or fat, which was rendered into a liquid that lit the lamps and greased the wheels of the world. One whale could yield twenty-five thousand tons of oil, and one toothless whale a ton of baleen!

Whaling made men rich. It was a tough, killing business, yet that didn't stop the whalers. The Basques were the first of the whalers, but they didn't come into much contact with the Greenlanders. A Basque vessel wrecked in 1745, however, probably gave Spaniol Island in Greenland its name. The Dutch did a lot of whaling in Greenland's waters—they sent nearly six thousand ships to Greenland within less than fifty years, more even than the British, French, and Americans.

Whaling voyages could last for years. The brief summer weeks that the water was open in Greenland were often not long enough for ships to make sufficient kills to pay for the journey. So the men would allow their ships to be frozen in and wait for the next year. Or, if they wanted to get home that year, they would gamble on one more day of whaling and then another and another . . . often to lose the gamble and awaken one morning to find themselves trapped in the pack ice. Sometimes they could free their ships by cutting the ice

Early print of whaling off the coast of Greenland.

with hatchets and pulling the boats through leads, paths of water between the ice floes, hoping that one of the leads would reach open water. If the leads gave out or the ice was too thick, there was nothing to do but spend the long winter aboard ship. With luck, the ship would stay in one piece—but not all ships were lucky.

The ice flocs, though hardly seeming to move, squeezed the wooden hulls, sometimes splintering them like nuts in a nutcracker. To keep from being crushed, the men might try to cut a channel in the ice around the boat. If breakup seemed inevitable, they would abandon ship, camp on the moving floes, and try to get to land. Land was also covered by ice, but at least on land they would not be moving helplessly in a current, vying for room with other floes that might up-end them at any moment. And on land they were in less danger from marauding polar bears, to whom the floes were home.

In the year 1777, an entire fleet of whaling ships was caught in pack ice off the east coast of Greenland. It was only the end of June, and the ships were taken completely by surprise. Sixteen of them worked free, but the rest were helpless in the ice. In mid-August, six of those that remained were crushed in one day. By the beginning of October five more were gone. Finally only one ship was left, carrying all 286 survivors. Food was rationed; the men were given ten tablespoons of weak soup or thin porridge a day. Drinking water was a terrible problem. Pack ice is sea ice and therefore salty; it cannot be drunk. The men had to search out the bergy bits, small pieces of iceberg moving in the pack ice. Iceberg ice comes from glaciers, which come from snow, and therefore it is drinkable when melted. But still the men died of thirst, starvation, and scurvy. And then the last ship was crushed.

The men divided into four groups. One went north and another went west. Neither was heard from again. A third group worked its way south and was eventually rescued by Eskimos. The fourth group stayed right where it was on the drifting pack ice. Carried by the East Greenland Current, which flows south and then west around the bottom of Greenland, the ice finally wound up on the west coast and the men were rescued.

The history of Greenland is full of stories similar to this one. Only the numbers change. In 1830, a record year for Greenland shipwrecks, eighteen ships in a fleet of whalers were crushed or swamped within fifteen minutes by a toppling iceberg. A thousand men were stranded on the pack ice, living in makeshift tents until other whalers could rescue them months later. This was the year remembered as the time the "whalers took a vacation," because they certainly didn't bring home any whales.

The Eskimos laughed at the whalers, but they accepted them. They traded for guns, which made hunting easier, and for iron pots, needles, and knives. They enjoyed Dutch genever, English gin, and American corn whiskey. And they raised children fathered by the whalers, so many children, in fact, that almost every family was of mixed blood, and the people of Greenland came to be called Greenlanders rather than Eskimos.

The Apostle of Greenland

The thought that there might be descendants of the Christian Norse in Greenland became an obsession with Hans Egede, a Lutheran pastor in Norway. Egede believed that without spiritual guidance, the Greenlanders' souls would be condemned to hell, and he was determined to find these unknowing Christians and bring them the solace of the religion of their ancestors. He pleaded with members of the Norwegian-Danish government to finance a mission to their Greenland colony.

The government was already uneasy that Dutch, French, English, and American whalers were casually making great profits in Greenland's waters. They saw Egede's mission as a way of colonizing land that belonged to them, land they had paid little attention to for three centuries and might now lose to some more aggressive nation interested in Greenland's resources. Sternly religious, the Danish-Norwegian king and his government were also unhappy about governing a land populated by heathens. So they agreed to send Pastor

Egede to Greenland, providing that he not only set up a Christian mission but also a colony with a trading post. A private trading company, the Bergen Company, was formed to carry on the Greenland trade and to finance the Greenland mission from its profits.

In 1721, Hans Egede sailed to Greenland with his wife, Gertrud Rasch, their sons Poul and Niels, and their daughters Kirstine and Pernill. With them went some forty others: carpenters, fishermen, stonemasons, coopers (makers of wooden barrels), an accountant, a

Hans Egede

Traditionally the Greenlanders carry their children in the hoods of their parkas.

[52]

surgeon, three women to do household chores, and the ship's crew to provide general labor. Their ship, the *Haabet,* or "Good Hope," anchored in a good harbor they named "Haabet Hevn," Harbor of Good Hope, on July 3, 1721. They chose an island in the harbor to settle on and named it Haabet, although Egede realized the exposed island location was a poor one. But winter was fast approaching and a shelter had to be built. Their shelter wasn't much—a three room house of turf and stone for about forty-five people. The Egede family lived in one room of that house for seven years.

Pastor Egede had gone to Greenland firm in the belief that he would understand the Greenlanders' language because it would be mixed with old Norse words. He also expected to find Christian beliefs, however distorted they might be by lack of spiritual guidance over the centuries. He did not find what he expected, although in later years he believed that he would have if he had understood their speech well enough to delve deeply into both language and beliefs.

The Greenlanders flocked to help build the Egede mission, but when they realized its people meant to stay, they were none too happy and took off. Undaunted by what he called their "coldness," Hans Egede worked to learn the language and took ever-lengthening journeys to trade and live with the Eskimos in their tents and houses. The journeys were cold and difficult, made on foot and in open boats in all kinds of weather. But most trying of all was living in the Greenlanders' homes. The odor was intolerable—not that the Europeans of the times lived odor-free. But twenty or more blubber lamps drying wet fur parkas and trousers, tubs of urine collecting for washing and medicinal purposes, and decaying meat waiting to be eaten made even the strongest of stomachs turn.

Pastor Egede also had a problem getting used to living with fifty or more naked people all around. The Greenlanders took off their heavy outdoor clothes when they went indoors, because their homes were tiny, airtight, and crowded with people whose 98.6 ° temperatures made effective heating units. Pastor Egede's greatest trial, however, was lice. He was tortured by the lice that infested the clothing and bodies of the Greenlanders. Crowded together as they were, unable to bathe in anything but a handful of melted snow or in urine, the Greenlanders accepted lice as an inevitable part of their lives. In fact, the Greenlanders made the best of the lice: they ate them. They also ate nasal discharges and sweat, which was carefully scraped from their bodies with an ivory or bone knife. Nothing could be wasted in a land where starvation always was possible if the weather became too bad to hunt or the prey became scarce.

Hans Egede could not discover any remnants of a European civilization among these people. He did not see evidence of Christianity in the religious practices of the angekoks, or medicine men. The angekoks exorcised evil spirits and enlisted the aid of spirits from under the sea or high in the mountains to relieve illness and insure good hunting. The angekoks were magicians, great escape artists and probably hypnotists who, among other things, could convince their audiences that they flew—rather like angels. But the angekoks were wise men. They readily admitted they did not know the secrets of the universe or of one god, and they did not prevent the Greenlanders from listening to the Christian missionaries.

Hans Egede, too, was a wise man, and a kind one. He nursed the ill and even seemed to perform a miracle when he washed a blind man's eyes with brandy and the man later regained his vision. Pastor Egede soon came to see that he could best bring his religion to these people by instructing the children. Poul, his son, went with him on many journeys, using Gospel scenes that he had drawn and colored to teach the children and any willing adults.

For all their belief in angekoks, the Greenlanders were a rational people, and they were eager to learn. They challenged the Egedes to explain, to teach more and more. Poul Egede translated the Lord's

The interior of a church in Greenland today. The church has an imposing presence in Greenland.

Prayer into the Greenlandic language, and "Give us this day our daily bread" became ". . . our daily meat," bread being unknown. Poul also translated the New Testament into Greenlandic—speaking Greenlandic came far more easily to the Egede children than to the parents.

The Egedes, and missionaries who later joined them, became schoolmasters, traveling the countryside, teaching children reading, writing, and religion. Arithmetic was entirely unnecessary in the Greenlandic hunting society. Greenlanders used a body system to count: first the fingers of the right hand, then of the left, then the right and left feet, and then a whole body as the unit for twenty.

The Greenlanders gathered wherever teaching was available, and the missionaries finally set up a system of catechists, Greenlanders trained by them to act as teachers. Wherever there was a catechist, settlements sprang up. Even a few Angmagssalik, the only Eskimos living on the east coast of Greenland and one step from the Stone Age, found their way around Cape Farewell and up to the missionaries. After their initial distrust, the Greenlanders had responded wholeheartedly to the missionaries. For what the missionaries preached surely must be important. Otherwise why would they have come so far and worked so hard to tell of it?

Egede was, nevertheless, very sparing in his conversions. He was rarely sure that the Greenlanders really embraced Christianity, for they were a gentle and kind people who politely told others whatever they seemed to want to hear. One of Pastor Egede's few baptisms was of a dying child brought to him by her angekok father, who desperately wanted her soul saved and at peace.

Hans Egede was not only a missionary, teacher, and trader, he was an explorer as well—if not by vocation, then by the necessity of having to seek out remote groups of Eskimos. He found the ruins of the Western Settlement not far from his own mission, and was determined to find the Eastern Settlement, which, along with every-

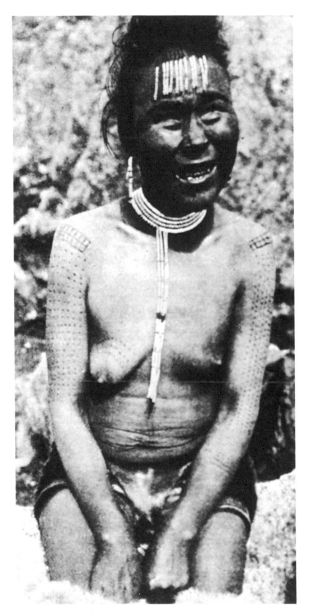

The east coast Greenlandic women at Angmagssalik
tatooed themselves up until the twentieth century.

body else, he believed to be on the east coast of Greenland. He had to give up any idea of climbing the mountains and crossing the ice sheet to reach the east coast, but he propounded a theory of reaching the east by umiak, or women's boat, a large skin boat rowed by the Greenland women. He was sure that the boat could navigate the ever-present ice moving south along the eastern coast and around Cape Farewell. Egede himself was never able to make the trip, but many years later his belief was proven correct. And actually, although he didn't know it, he didn't need to get to the east coast: Egede had *found* the ruins of the Eastern Settlement south of the ruins of the Western Settlement, to which he thought they belonged.

As a trader, Egede did not fare so well. Not many ships could make the voyage from Norway, and many of those that did were lost in storms. Lotteries were set up in Norway and Denmark to benefit the Bergen Company and the Egede mission. Everyone except the peasants had to buy tickets. But by 1726, with the loss of still another ship, the Bergen Company was forced to give up. The Egede mission faced starvation, and King Frederik IV of Norway-Denmark ordered another lottery to help them. The king also sent five ships of supplies and people to help colonize Greenland. The people were prisoners from the king's jails, however, along with soldiers to guard them. They arrived in Greenland in 1728 and moved the Egede mission from Haabat Island to the settlement they established on the mainland at Godthaab. The male prisoners were made to draw lots for the names of female prisoners who would become their wives. For the king it was a happy solution—he was rid of people who were crowding his jails (he hoped eventually to send more over), and he was populating a country that would reward him with increased trade and prosperity.

For Greenland it was less than a happy situation. Picking a wife by lottery offered little guarantee of contentment. Many a new wife was flogged for being "disrespectful," and the soldiers' wives and children did not fare much better. Brutality, fighting, and drunkenness were common. Even the royal governor, Claus Paars, Greenland's first and only military governor, had at least one drunken brawl over a woman, and that with the commander of the troops!

The Greenlanders could not understand this kind of thing at all. Wives were expected to be helpful and faithful to their husbands, although if the need arose, or there was a party, a wife could be shared. A woman who could mend a kayak or a kamak (boot) was essential on the hunt, and if a wife could not make the journey, someone else's wife was gladly loaned for the purpose. Selfishness, thieving, brutality, and brawling were not the Eskimo way.

Governor Claus Paars did his best to keep order, but he was ineffective. Governor Paars did manage to become the first known European to stand on the Greenland ice sheet, however. The king had directed Paars to cross the ice to look for the Eastern Settlement. With much difficulty, Paars and his men and the horses they brought for the journey made it up the mountains and onto the ice sheet. But the horses died of cold and hunger almost immediately, and after walking a few hours the men reached their first crevasse. They looked. Then they sat down on the ice, drank a toast to the health of the king, and went home to Godthaab.

The Eskimos of the Godthaab region were increasing in number, drawn to the mission by the opportunity to be with people, the church services, and the chance to save their souls. But the society the Norwegian-Danish brought to Greenland was unhappy, violent, and oppressive. A society in which there were governors and governed, people who had to be kept in order by force, was completely foreign to the Eskimo. Pastor Egede had preached his church's stern morality to the Greenlanders, and they had listened, even though some of the things he preached against had not seemed bad or sinful. But now they saw that the pastor's own people did not practice what was preached. So what right had these foreigners to tell the

Greenlanders have always enjoyed making music. Here a modern choral group in traditional dress makes a guest appearance.

Greenlanders, a reasonable and rational people, how to live and behave?

Not only were the Greenlanders in rebellion—the convicts and the troops were dismayed at the harshness of their lives. They demonstrated their anger by besieging the mission. Officers of the military had to guard Egede's home against attack. Scurvy, starvation, and murder eventually took care of the soldiers and the convicts, and the first—and last—military government of Greenland was recalled.

Although the Greenlanders seem to have been more civilized than the Europeans, the "heathens" were still the object of concern to many missionary Christians in Europe. A small group of German missionaries from the Moravian Brethren decided to bring their religion to Greenland. They set up business only a short distance from the Egede mission and drew many Greenlanders into their fold. The Greenlanders loved the small organ the Moravians had brought, and their singing, but they were sadly disappointed that dancing was forbidden. Still, the Greenlanders seemed to prefer the Moravians, who offered conversion more easily than the Egedes, a conversion that they eagerly sought for the good of their souls.

The Egedes could not help but be disappointed that their mission—and their trading company—was failing in comparison with the Moravians, who were far better funded. Indeed, the Moravians were causing something of a problem in Godthaab, and not only on a personal level. In the Moravian church, attendance was required at two services a day. The Greenlanders in the Moravian fold, known as the "German Greenlanders," found little time for much else, including essential hunting. How far from town could you go when you had to be home twice a day to attend prayer meetings? Nor were the Egede missionaries blameless. To simplify their tasks of trade and Christianizing, they encouraged the Greenlanders to congregate in one place, and that place soon became overhunted.

Supply ships were infrequent, so when the hunting was poor, the people went hungry.

Worse still, town living generated epidemics. Influenza, measles, and smallpox, brought from Europe by whalers, explorers, missionaries, traders, and returning Greenlanders, devastated the Greenlanders, who had little or no immunity. Disease struck house after house with nothing to stop its progress. In 1736, a terrible epidemic of smallpox broke out in the Godthaab area, introduced by a Greenlander who had visited Denmark. Between two and three thousand people died before the epidemic was over. The missionaries expended all their energies nursing the sick. Gertrud Rasch, exhausted by it, died in 1738.

This was one hardship too many for Hans Egede. He left Greenland with the body of his wife and never returned, even when he was ordained bishop of Greenland. Poul and Niels Egede continued his work in Greenland, as did two of Hans Egede's nephews. Egede himself established the Greenland Seminary in Denmark for training missionaries.

Greenland's existence as a Danish country is due to Hans Egede's colonization efforts and his long voyages to its remote areas. Colonization in later years was carried out according to principles Pastor Egede laid down, and the trust of the Greenlanders was won by the goodness of the Egedes and their hard work. But the Egedes never knew the taste of success—they only knew they had fallen short of their goals of converting all of Greenland and of creating a flourishing trade and a Europen culture there. What would Hans Egede make of the fact that today he is called "the Apostle of Greenland"?

Closed Country—Open World

When Hans Egede returned from Greenland he was cared for by a man named Jakob Severin, a businessman who for sixteen years tried to keep up the work of the Egedes by developing the Greenland trade. The Norwegian-Danish government had given Severin a trade monopoly—the right to *all* Greenland trade—in 1734. In return, Severin had to give an annual sum of money to the Egede missions. Although Neils Egede was a fine trader, the mission had not made a success of the Greenland trade, largely because of competition from the Dutch, who sent some seventy ships a year into Greenland, trading pots, pans, trinkets, and toys for furs.

Now, however, Severin barred Dutch ships as well as ships of other countries from Greenland's waters. The Dutch did not like this one bit and sent five armored ships to the tiny Greenland settlement at Maklyout, north of Godthaab, to force entrance to the harbor. The Dutch ships found seven of Severin's ships waiting for them. Exactly at midnight of the day the ban on foreign shipping went into effect, Severin's ships opened fire. An hour later, the Dutch honorably surrendered, and everybody retreated to shore for a different kind of battle: to see who could drink the most. Maklyout was renamed Jakobshaven in honor of Jakob Severin, and Poul Egede built a mission there.

Severin did not make the Greenland trade any more profitable than previous companies had. Weather conditions were so bad, epidemics so devastating, that the supply of furs, tusks, and other Greenland products was limited. Supply ships had trouble reaching port and had little to bring back.

So, in 1776, the Danish-Norwegian government took over the job of supplying all of Greenland's needs in exchange for all of her trade items. They closed Greenland to all private trade—the beginning of a 176-year period during which Greenland remained shut off to the world. All ships in Greenland's waters had to submit to the right of search and seizure. And no one was allowed to take a Greenlander out of the country or do any other violence to the natives.

The Danish-Norwegian government set up a trading company, "The Royal Greenland, Iceland, Finnmark and Faroe Trading Company," later simply "The Royal Greenland Trading Company," to take care of Greenland's needs. The Company was not merely a business. Its trading posts were also the means of governing Greenland, which was now divided into two provinces, North and South Greenland. North and South were each headed by an inspector, who was also a general manager of the Royal Greenland Trading Company. The inspectors acted as chiefs of police and judges for their respective territories. Every settlement was given a trading post with a shopkeeper who administered all the affairs of the settlement. The shopkeeper in turn had several assistants, some of whom acted as policemen. The shopkeepers and their assistants were usually ordinary seamen formerly in the China trade. Many were drunkards, mean and quarrelsome, particularly in the smaller settlements where food was poor and wages so low that the men could never save enough to leave. Only the lower ranks were allowed to marry Greenlanders, and discontent was rampant.

The Greenlanders were now being governed by policemen, managers, and missionaries, all of whom were meshed together into one network that controlled supplies, religion, and lives. Greenlanders had had no chiefs, no leaders. The closest they came to the idea of a ruler was when the best hunter assumed the role of leader for a brief period, perhaps when the meat he brought in had to be divided among the people. Now in some settlements like Frederikshaab, the manager of the trading company set himself up almost as a god, and the missionary was not very far below him, demanding attendance at both midnight and 6:00 A.M. services. Elsewhere in the villages the churches required attendance at morning and evening prayers, as well as at Sunday services, or fines were inflicted. Laughter in church was also fined or punished by beatings—saving souls became an ugly business.

Why the Greenlanders submitted to such treatment is puzzling. A nomadic people, they could have moved. Perhaps they reasoned that the missionaries would just seek them out and urge them into villages again, as they had before. And the Greenlanders enjoyed town life, with its opportunities for socializing. Towns also meant easy access to the trader's coffee, tea, sugar, and tobacco, which the Greenlanders had come to crave in their diets. They had no milk, but instead sometimes whipped an egg into sweetened coffee for a delicious drink. Eggs from the eider duck and various other Arctic birds were plentiful.

To its credit, the government tried to prevent these European influences from interfering with the Greenlanders' native lifestyle. It encouraged them to keep their own foods, their own ways. At one point Greenlanders were even *forbidden* European food except in times of famine or illness, a measure designed to force them to hunt.

This policy was essential not only to Greenlanders' culture, but also to their health, well-being, food supply, and clothing. It was essential to the well-being of the Europeans, too, whose supplies ran low between ships.

In an article for a Copenhagen newspaper, an inspector, the highest-ranking official in Greenland, wrote that all "Proper Meals" included a brush he had invented for removing the mold from hardtack, a long-lasting cracker used as emergency rations on ships and in frontier countries. Hardtack in Greenland became known as "sneezing bread," because the inspector's brush caused the mold to fly into eyes and noses.

This was a harsh country for Europeans, particularly if they could not or would not adjust to Eskimo foods. Scurvy, a disease caused by the lack of Vitamin C found in many fresh vegetables and fruits, killed many Europeans in Greenland. The Greenlanders did not suffer from scurvy because their regular diets contained certain grasses, which the Europeans disdained, not realizing their therapeutic value.

When their people died in Greenland, the Royal Greenland Trading Company simply sent out more, and so did the Lutherans and Moravians. Greenland did not change. Even when the Norwegian-Danish Union was split up, Greenland did not change. Norway was taken away from Denmark in 1815, when the Congress of Vienna tallied up the wins and losses of the Napoleonic Wars. Denmark had sided with Napoleon and was therefore a loser. Oddly enough, no one at the Congress of Vienna remembered the Greenland colony, so it remained by default with Denmark. Denmark continued the administration of the Royal Greenland Trading Company, and Greenland hardly felt the impact of the Congress of Vienna.

In the mid-1800s, a Moravian missionary who lost his religious vocation and became a virtual hermit, *did* bring change to Greenland. Samuel Kleinschmidt, a scholar, developed an alphabet for the

Greenlandic language, so that for the first time it could be written down. The alphabet had a Roman base but did not have the letter "C." Kleinschmidt also set up a printing press, and soon the Greenlanders had a weekly newspaper and a magazine.

Still, Greenland remained a hunting society closed to the world, protected from outsiders by the Royal Greenland Trading Company. And yet Greenland's geography put her in the middle of world affairs. On the other side of the world, the Russians were on

Title page of a Greenlandic spelling book, illustrated by a Greenlander.

the move. Vitus Bering, a Dane working for the Tsar of Russia, had explored the waters between the Asian and North American continents in the mid-eighteenth century. Bering discovered the sea route between the continents in 1740, sighting the Alaska coast and opening the American continent to Russian settlement as far south as San Francisco. This made the Spanish nervous about their California settlements, and it made the British nervous about their territory of Canada and their hopes for the fur trade along the Pacific coast.

A speedy sea route across the top of the world to the Pacific Ocean was considered essential to stop Russian encroachment. The search for the Northwest Passage, neglected for many years, was on again. And Greenland figured in most of the expeditions.

John Ross, a Briton, headed several such expeditions at the beginning of the nineteenth century. He did not find the Northwest Passage, but he did discover a tribe of Eskimos in the far north of Greenland, the Polar Eskimos, who thought they were the only human beings in the world. After all, they had never seen any other men. How does an explorer approach such a people? John Ross had a flag made showing an outstretched hand, and hung it from his ship's mast. The Eskimos responded with *their* sign of friendship: they all pulled their noses. It was fortunate that they made friends, for Ross's expedition was marooned for four years in that far northern ice. Without the help of the Polar Eskimos probably no one would have survived.

Ross made another voyage to find the Northwest Passage, but he suddenly turned back, claiming he saw mountains in the distance that would block his way. There were no mountains, and Ross was accused of lying and branded a coward. Having been marooned in the ice four years, Ross may perhaps be excused a little cowardice, if that is what it was. But probably he saw a mirage, an optical illusion. Mirages are common in cold Arctic waters, when certain temperature differences between water and air cause light to be reflected at a higher angle than normal, and objects beyond the horizon seem in a straight line from the viewer. Or at a certain point a mirror effect can take place, sometimes upside down as well as in reverse, and the viewer sees before him what is actually behind or beside him. There is a theory that Leif Ericson reached Vinland because of a series of mirages; but others rebut this theory, arguing that in Leif's day the climate was warmer and mirages were therefore less likely.

Ocean mirages were not well understood in the nineteenth century, however, and John Ross was not absolved of cowardice. His second-in-command, Edward Perry, was put in charge of Britain's next expedition to discover the Northwest Passage. Perry became famous in the annals of Arctic exploration as the man who pushed his way into far nothern Canada, across the icy waters from Greenland.

But John Ross was not yet through. He led another expedition into Greenland waters, an expedition that became famous for the discovery by his nephew, James Clark Ross, of the magnetic north pole. Not to be confused with the geographic north pole, where all the lines of longitude come together, the magnetic north pole is where the needles of all compasses point. When you get there, the compass needle should point straight down, which of course it cannot do. So it goes slightly mad and swings off 90 degrees, becoming unusable. And, as if this were not confusing enough to a navigator, the magnetic north pole is not stationary—it moves northeastward about six miles per year. There is also a magnetic south pole which behaves in the same fashion. *And* there are two poles of inaccessibility, centers of rotation of the Arctic and Antarctic ice packs.

Impressed by his discovery of the magnetic north pole, the British offered James Clark Ross an expedition of his own to search for the Northwest Passage. He refused, and the expedition was headed instead by Sir John Franklin, a hero of the Battle of Trafalgar, in which the British crushed Napoleon's navy. Sir John set off for Greenland's waters in 1845, with two ships, the *Erebus* and the *Terror,* 128 men, a band, and supplies for four years. Sir John did not want to take chances on running out of food. On a previous expedition to the Arctic he had seen his men eat one sailor and try to kill others for that purpose. Sir John was ill-fated. This expedition, too, was to meet with cannibalism.

This Franklin expedition is probably the most famous and in a way the most important Arctic expedition of all, not because of what it accomplished, for it accomplished nothing, but because it disappeared. In response to frantic pleas from Lady Franklin, over forty relief expeditions went to Greenland and Canada to try to find Sir John and his men. Some of the expeditions got into trouble in the ice and were themselves the subject of searches. The Danish government cooperated by allowing the searchers into Greenland, and a huge body of knowledge about the Arctic and Greenland made its way into maps and geography books. The fate of the Franklin Expedition itself was not learned until years later, when John Rae in 1854 and Sir Francis McClintock in 1859 found records of Franklin's death in 1847, and the abandonment of the ships in the ice in 1848. Not one member of the crew survived the trek over the ice toward civilization. Relics and documents were being found as late as 1960, and the search for Franklin's diaries is still going on today.

In 1853, during the Franklin searches, the Northwest Passage was finally discovered, almost accidentally, by Robert McClure of the British Royal Navy. McClure did not travel the Passage, but he demonstrated its existence by linking up a sea and land route to a route Edward Perry had charted some thirty years earlier. It was not until 1903-06 that Roald Amundsen became the first person to travel the Northwest Passage all the way from Europe to the Pacific. Ironically, by then the magic Passage had little value for commerce or defense, and the world had lost interest.

Heinrich J. Rink

Another interest had taken its place—the theory of an ice age in which the world was covered with ice. The theory had been proposed in the 1840s, and scientist-explorers came to the Greenland ice sheet to try to understand what a world covered in ice would have been like. Heinrich Rink, a Danish scientist, artist, and self-taught expert on Eskimo culture, studied and wrote much about the Greenland ice sheet. Rink called it the "inland ice," a term most Greenlanders used, and described how the ice must have formed, moved, and covered the world, leaving behind the moraine it carried when it retreated. Rink loved Greenland and in 1853 became manager of the colony at Julienhaab and superintendent of South Greenland. Ill health forced Rink to return to Denmark, where he became chairman of the Royal Greenland Trading Company—probably the only man in Greenland's history to understand it so well in so many ways.

Rink made the Greenland ice sheet world famous, and men came to study and to conquer it. They even investigated laying the transatlantic cable across it—and decided instead to go under the ocean; that looked easier. In 1876, a Commission for Geological and Geographical Investigations in Greenland was formed to organize all the research going on.

Many people of the time believed there was at least one oasis of ice-free land on the ice sheet and that it might be inhabited—possibly by descendants of the lost Norse. The Commission sponsored several expeditions to the ice sheet. But even unsuccessful expeditions served a purpose: they showed what would and would not work in the way of transportation and equipment, and what was necessary in the way of supplies. The last of the Commission's expeditions, led in 1878 by Lt. J.A.D. Jensen, brought back drawings that for the first time showed the world what the inland ice sheet looked like, arousing international interest.

Another failed expedition was led by the explorer A.E. Nordenskjold in 1881, just one year after he discovered and navigated the Northeast Passage to great acclaim. However, Nordenskjold confirmed that the dangerous crevasses—the ones that had so frightened Claus Paars and his men—were confined to the borders of the ice sheet. The interior of the ice sheet, Nordenskjold said, was smooth. He was unable to cross it because he had mounted his expedition at a time when the surface of the ice had turned to slush, causing men and equipment to sink down. Only two Laplanders on the expedition, experts on skis, were able to navigate the slush.

Skis were not as well known in those days as now, but their proven success on an expedition confirmed the decision of Fridtjof Nansen, a Norwegian scientist-explorer, to use them in his attempt to cross the inland ice. Nansen copied from another expedition also, one in which Robert E. Peary fitted his sledge with a sail and, using skis and ski poles as masts, sailed over the ice.

Nansen was not simply a follower, he was also an innovator. He came up with a new approach to conquering the ice sheet—his party would start from the *east* coast and cross to the west, rather than the other way around as all previous expeditions had attempted. Nansen reasoned that west-to-east expeditions had to carry enough supplies for a return journey to civilization. Since there was nothing to return to on the east coast, his expedition would need to make only a one-way crossing.

The problem was getting to the east coast in the first place. The ice-bound east coast had intimidated sailors from Eric the Red on. It still does, to this day. But in the early 1800s, a British whaler by the name of William Scoresby had made the first landing on the east coast, and had compiled a wealth of information on water temperatures and depths. Now Nansen and five companions sailed from Norway to the east coast of Greenland, disembarked in the pack ice, and set out in small boats to cross the floes to land. But they were frozen in and drifted far south of where they wanted to be. Eventually they walked over floes and kayaked through leads toward the north, finally making it to land. The men had tremendous difficulty raising their equipment up the mountains onto the ice sheet, but once they reached it they had little trouble crossing. Actually, their greatest problem was thirst.

On that vast expanse of snow—for that matter, throughout the Arctic—drinking water was and is a problem. There is no groundwater to supply wells and springs, as there is in most other areas of the world. In the Arctic, the ground, called "permafrost," is permanently frozen. Meltwater pools form on the ice sheet in summer, but travel in summer is impossible because slush also forms.

To get drinking water ice had to be melted, but for that heat was needed, and fuel was precious. Carrying fuel was cumbersome, so the amount was always closely calculated. If more had to be used for heating and cooking than had been anticipated, a problem arose.

The waterworks at Frederikshaab. There is no groundwater in
Greenland, so water is obtained either from natural lakes or by damming
rivers, or melting ice.

The success of an expedition might depend on something as simple
as a stove that used fuel efficiently. The Greenlanders could have
taught Nansen their ways of surviving on long expeditions, but the
Greenlanders would not travel on the inland ice.

Their sufferings from thirst proved of little consequence when the
men finally reached the west coast at Ameralik Fjord, south of
Godthaab. Anxious to tell the world of their feat, they fashioned a
boat from osier branches they found in the valley and made sails of

their canvas tent floors. Nansen and another member of the expedition sailed and rowed their way to Godthaab, arriving just after the last boat had left Greenland. So word of crossing the Greenland ice sheet did not reach the world until the following spring, 1889. The news brought Nansen world fame comparable to the recognition given the early astronauts.

Nansen lived up to that fame, as a scientist, an explorer, a diplomat, and a humanitarian.

He had a theory that a current ran across the top of the world from Siberia to Greenland. He based his theory on several pieces of evidence that seemed clear to him but not to many other people. One was the large amount of driftwood and mud washed up on Greenland's shores around Jakobshaven. Nansen felt the driftwood could only have come from the great forests of eastern Siberia. Another piece of evidence was a "throwing stick" found on a beach in Greenland but of a type used by the Siberian Eskimos to kill birds. And a third important clue was a scrap of paper, a list of supplies signed by U. S. Navy Lieutenant George Washington DeLong. De-Long, commander of the *Jeannette,* had tried in 1879 to reach the North Pole by way of the Bering Strait. The ship had been frozen in, and he and his men had tried to reach Siberia by crossing the pack ice by boat and on foot. But they died of cold and starvation in 1881. Two years later DeLong's list turned up on the other side of the world, in Greenland. Nansen reasoned that only a current could have brought it there.

To test his theory, Nansen decided to allow a ship to be frozen into the pack ice off Siberia to see where it would drift. He had a ship built with a special hull three feet thick and sloping, so that ice pressing against it would squeeze the ship upward, allowing it to ride the ice instead of being crushed. Nansen and his crew sailed the ship, the *Fram,* into the pack ice off Siberia and waited to be frozen in. The *Fram* drifted with the ice, moved by the current that Nansen had theorized must exist. After two years of drifting, Nansen decided the ship was not going to drift exactly across the North Pole—and he wanted to reach the Pole. So he and a companion, Hjalmar Johansen, got out and started walking. They carried their supplies on sledges. Only 270 miles from the Pole they encountered unpassable ledges of ice and had to turn back.

Nansen and Johansen worked their way toward land—what land, they didn't know. They found out later that they were in Franz Josef's Land (now, appropriately enough, called Fridtjof Nansen's Land). One day in June, just as they were running low on food, a man appeared out of nowhere. He was well dressed, shaven, a civilized man who politely raised the hat he was wearing and said, "How do you do?" Nansen recognized a fellow explorer, Frederick G. Jackson. Jackson did not recognize the wild-looking man confronting him as the world-famous Nansen. Hesitating to seem forward, Jackson inquired if there was a boat nearby. No, no boat, replied Dr. Nansen. The civilities finally ended when the overly polite Jackson realized to whom he was speaking and allowed himself a more excited, open welcome. Nansen, on the other hand, was impressed that Jackson had been *so* polite to a stranger! Men of the nineteenth century had rather fixed ideas about etiquette, even in the middle of thousands of miles of nothing but snow and ice.

Nansen and Johansen sailed back to Norway on the boat that brought supplies to Jackson's expedition. They arrived, almost miraculously, on the same day that the *Fram* broke out of the pack ice, having drifted, as Nansen had predicted, across the top of the world. Eight days later Nansen and his men on the *Fram* were reunited in Norway. Newspapers around the world heralded their feat with wild excitement.

Nansen had not succeeded in reaching the North Pole, but his highly detailed observations of currents, polar ice drift, and methods of Arctic survival laid the basis for all future Arctic work.

He went on to become an honored statesman, who helped bring about the separation of Sweden from Norway, and he became the first Norwegian minister to Great Britain. Nansen was internationally acclaimed for his efforts to relieve the great famine in Russia just after World War I and for his repatriation of war prisoners and refugees. He devised the Nansen Passport for these stateless people,

Nansen (middle row, second from right, in porkpie hat) surrounded by the crew of the Fram.

since they could neither travel nor settle without papers. For all these things, Fridtjof Nansen received the Nobel Peace Prize in 1922.

These Arctic explorers who belong to Greenland's history were extraordinary men who did extraordinary things. They had no radios, no radar, no steel ships, no planes, no knowledge of the nutritional necessities of life, no antibiotics. They suffered terrible rheumatism, snowblindness, starvation, and frostbite—losing fingers, toes, legs, and lives as gangrene set in from blocked circulation. All to achieve a dream, a dream of understanding and conquering nature.

Soon after Nansen crossed the ice sheet, the American explorer Robert E. Peary crossed Greenland for the first time to the far north, north of the ice sheet, in what is now Pearyland. He reached the northern borders of Greenland and confirmed that the country was an island surrounded by sea ice. Peary made several more expeditions to the far north of Greenland, where he found three important meteorites—one weighing thirty-six and a half tons. All three are now displayed at the Hayden Planetarium in New York City. Peary's expeditions also demonstrated that Arctic expeditions need not lose lives or cost extravagant amounts. There was universal distaste growing for the loss of life in the Arctic on mostly failed expeditions. Peary also showed that these expeditions need not be uncivilized: several included his wife, Josephine, who gave birth to their daughter while wintering in Greenland above the Arctic Circle. Still, Arctic expeditions had their problems. Peary himself fractured a leg, got frostbite, and had to have seven toes amputated with a scissors to prevent gangrene.

Peary's later expeditions were designed as practice runs for his dream of being the first man to reach the North Pole. Peary's initial try was a failure, but on April 6, 1909, he realized his dream. Accompanied by four Polar Eskimos and Matthew Henson, his black servant, Peary made the dash for the Pole from the last of a set of relay

Robert E. Peary

stations put up along the way to care for the six men so they could make the final push in the best possible condition.

But when Peary announced his feat, he found that Dr. Frederick Cook, a member of one of his early expeditions, was also claiming to have reached the North Pole and was being given a hero's welcome

Dr. Cook at a dinner in his honor after he announced his discovery of the North Pole.

in Europe and America. A huge scandal erupted. A disillusioned public made fun of the explorers, the Arctic, Greenland, the Eskimos—quite the opposite of what Peary hoped to achieve. It was some time before Peary's claim was upheld, but even today doubts and questions remain.

A well-known Greenland figure, the journalist and explorer Peter Freuchen, was one of the people to fight Cook's claims. Freuchen, a Dane, managed the Cape York Station Thule, a trading post in the northernmost settlement in Greenland, that of the Polar Eskimos. The Thule trading post had been started as a private enterprise by Freuchen's friend Knud Rasmussen. Rasmussen was a Greenlander, the son of a Jakobshaven pastor and a Danish-Eskimo mother. He had started the trading post in order to help the Eskimos with whom he had spent most of his life, and he also wanted to secure thé area for Denmark. Traders, whalers, and explorers seemed to regard northern Greenland as international territory. In fact, the United States didn't recognize Danish sovereignty in Greenland at all until 1917, when Denmark sold the Danish Virgin Islands in the Caribbean to the United States. And as late as 1924, the danger of a divided Greenland became very real: Norway gave Norwegian hunters power of possession in uninhabited areas of Greenland. Denmark finally had to appeal to the International Court at the Hague, and that body ruled in 1933 that the *whole* of Greenland belonged to Denmark.

Rasmussen's move to set up a trading post had been a wise one. He was a perceptive, intelligent man, as well as a great explorer and a writer. Rasmussen and Peter Freuchen joined an expedition led by Ludwig Mylius-Erichsen, another writer. Their journey of exploration in northern Greenland from 1902–1904 became famous as the Danish Literary Greenland Expedition because of its literary members. Mylius-Erichsen was to die in 1908 on a mapping expedition in the far north of Greenland. The men who went out to recover his

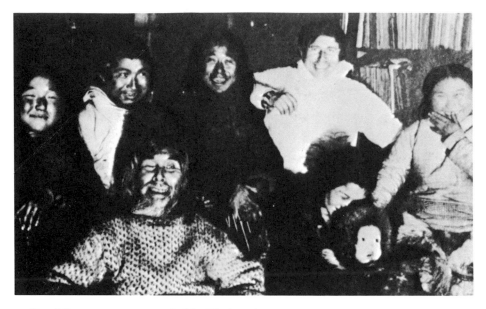

Knud Rasmussen surrounded by Thule Eskimos.

body became lost, however, so Rasmussen and Freuchen set out in 1912 to find them and also to map the north. This was the first of seven Thule Expeditions, named for their point of departure, and famous in the annals of Arctic exploration.

Other Thule Expeditions crossed the north to survey and to search for archeological evidence of the pre-Eskimo cultures and their routes of migration from the north to the south of Greenland. Freuchen lost a leg to frostbite and gangrene on one of the expeditions, and an Eskimo hunter was lost during a hunting trip on another expedition on the ice sheet, which almost killed them all. Hunting was poor, and Rasmussen depended on hunting and living Eskimo style rather than on hauling food supplies, as was the practice on other expeditions. The sledge dogs had to be killed and eaten—not uncommon in the Arctic and often the reason for using

Knud Rasmussen (right) and Earl Rossman. The photograph was taken on the trail where they met during the Fifth Thule Expedition.

dogs to haul sledges rather than having men pull them by rope. The expedition's footgear was worn through, and the routes over the crevasses on the outskirts of the ice were filled with waist-deep water. Sledges were abandoned, and one of the men, unable to go any further, also had to be abandoned so the others could go on to safety.

Rasmussen never went out on the ice sheet again. But he had added greatly to the scientific understanding of the ice sheet, and Peter Freuchen had described for the first time the way the ice sheet was layered. This led later scientists to make core drillings to study the layers, learning how they showed the weather over past centuries. These and still other expeditions gave scientists knowledge and procedures for studying the ice sheet in Antarctica.

The Fifth Thule Expedition became the most famous. Also called "The Long Sledge Journey," it lasted three years and covered twenty-four thousand miles from Greenland across Canada to the Pacific Ocean. It was designed to study the Eskimo. Rasmussen found that all the Eskimo groups he met could understand much of his Greenlandic speech, confirming for him that the Eskimos of the world had a common origin, had once all spoken the same language. The Fifth Thule Expedition brought home thousands of items displaying the history and culture of the Eskimo. These are now housed in the National Museum in Copenhagen, Denmark, and have aroused the awareness and gained the respect of the world for the culture of the Eskimo, the Inuit.

Wars, Spies, and Atomic Cities

World War I put an end for a time to all the Greenland expeditions—money and manpower were needed for the war. Greenland had no place in the fighting. But the war had shown the military importance of the airplane and of getting the airplane to combat areas quickly. An air route over Greenland was under serious discussion in Great Britain, Germany, and the United States. If planes were to fly over Greenland's ice sheet, more had to be known about the climate there year-round. So the end of World War I marked the beginning of modern geophysical research in the Arctic.

Detailed observations of weather, wind conditions, altitudes, and ice conditions were conducted by the British and the Germans in the center of the ice sheet, and by the Americans on the west coast at Sondre Stromfjord just above the Arctic Circle. By 1931, experimental air flights were being made over the ice sheet.

Scientific expeditions were conducted all over Greenland, measuring, mapping, digging for archeological findings, analyzing snow, water, ice, air, mountains, graves, plant life, and animal life.

And then, in 1939, it all stopped. War enveloped the world.

On September 1, 1939, Hitler's armies invaded Poland. Two days later England and France declared war on Germany. Canada and the rest of the British Commonwealth (except Ireland) joined the war. The Nazis were threatening Norway and Denmark. Canada was fearful that Denmark would soon fall to the Nazis, who would then be able to use Greenland as a base of operations against her. The Canadians wanted to occupy Greenland before the Germans had a chance to, but the United States would not allow it. President Franklin D. Roosevelt invoked the Monroe Doctrine, which declared that the United States would not allow any foreign government to interfere with any country on the American continent, to warn Canada away from Greenland.

The United States had long been aware that the country that held Greenland could dominate the Atlantic. During the Civil War, Secretary of State William Seward, who purchased Alaska from the Russians, had also wanted to buy Greenland, Iceland, and Jan Mayen, a Norwegian island in the North Atlantic, to protect the North American continent. But "Seward's Folly"—Alaska—was as much as the government could handle at the time. Now the United States was faced with the Canadian assumption of power over Greenland and thus possible postwar control by a British Commonwealth nation.

Canada stayed away from Greenland, but President Roosevelt ordered five Coast Guard cutters to Greenland to transport Greenland and U.S. State Department officials, to bring in supplies, to establish good will among the Greenlanders, and to survey the coast. The cutters also brought former U.S. Coast Guardsmen to stand watch over the small cryolite mine at Ivigtut. Cryolite is a mineral used in

The cryolite mine.

making baking soda, and the mine was considered of little value—
until cryolite became vital to aluminum production and aluminum
vital to airplane construction.

President Roosevelt also sent a top secret expedition of army,
navy, and Coast Guard personnel to Greenland to survey sites for
building airfields and weather stations. The utmost secrecy was ob-
served because the United States was still officially a neutral country, and the government was assuring Americans that they would

An outpost of the Greenland Patrol on the east coast during World War II.

[88]

not be going to war. But Roosevelt knew that the United States would soon be part of the war and that control of Greenland was vital for ferrying planes, reporting weather conditions, and preventing the Nazis from getting too close.

The top secret expedition to Greenland was started in March, 1941, under cover of the International Ice Patrol. The Ice Patrol was funded by many countries, although it was administered by the U.S. Coast Guard, so it made a perfect cover. Barely one month later, just as Canada and the United States had feared, Denmark signed a non-aggression pact with Germany, camouflage for a Nazi takeover. The Danish ambassador to the United States was recalled, but he ignored the summons and quickly signed an agreement on behalf of the Danish government for the United States and Canada to protect and provision Greenland in return for cryolite.

Although the United States was still not at war, things were looking pretty warlike out there. German U-boats were operating successfully right off her Atlantic coast, and the Greenland-bound task force had at one point to be diverted to rescue torpedoed merchantmen and British sailors. And now there were Americans occupying a colony belonging to a country occupied by the Nazis! When the Americans arrived in Greenland they found the country dotted with Danish hunting shacks, almost every one already set up as a radio station relaying information about the constantly changing weather to Denmark and the Nazis. A Greenland Patrol made up of Greenlanders, Danes, and United States naval men (the navy by then included Coast Guardsmen, a merger traditional in wartime) was organized to search out the Germans and the ships that were supplying them. One of the patrols made the first naval capture of World War II for the United States—three months before official United States entrance into the war. A Norwegian trawler (the Nazis had conquered Norway just after the pact with Denmark) was seized, along with the radio station it was servicing on shore.

When the United States entered the war on December 8, 1941, the Greenland Patrol was given added muscle. Ten civilian fishing trawlers were drafted right out of Boston harbor and christened with Greenlandic names for animals. One of them, the *Natsek*, was lost with all hands on December 17, 1942, probably gunned down by Germans in a remote Greenland fjord.

The Greenlanders now relied on Americans for the supplies they needed. The United States had to convoy food, clothing, lumber for building, fishing nets, and hundreds of other civilian goods along with military supplies for the Greenland patrol and the naval and air force personnel there.

Greenland duty was tough and dangerous. Besides fog, storms, and ice, ships faced attacks from U-boats. When they could fly, planes covered the convoys. An average of fifty-four planes a day made antisubmarine sweeps, weather and ice reports, and rescue flights. They also delivered the mail. In every village, one official building, usually the warehouse of the Royal Greenland Trading Company, had a large tile number on its roof to guide navigators of the planes. Most are still in place today. Using code, guard ships stationed in the waters off the coast radioed planes to warn of local weather changes—the weather changed frequently and sometimes dangerously for aircraft. And when the Germans broke the code, it was dangerous too. Two Flying Fortresses with four fighter escorts were radioed from one airfield to another, each one reporting that the weather was too bad to permit landing, until the planes were forced down for lack of fuel. Miraculously, all six planes landed safely on the ice sheet, and the twenty-five flyers walked off unhurt, eventually to discover that the Germans had broken the code and were responsible for forcing them down. Weather conditions at the fields had been adequate for landing all along.

The planes were all lost—perhaps one of the bombers was the one that the Ice Patrol spotted years later entombed in an iceberg. But

Coastguardsmen capture twelve Nazis at a radio weather station in Greenland.

many other planes also went down on the ice sheet. In 1942, a Flying Fortress crashed in a whiteout, a condition where ice and sky are one color. A pilot cannot see a horizon and is without any visual points of reference to keep him from flying into the ground if his instruments are not functioning properly. A rescue plane was sent out to pick up the bomber's crew. It landed on the ice sheet and two men were brought out safely. But when the rescue plane returned for the remaining crew, it too crashed, and all aboard were killed.

The airbase directing rescue operations sent out two more men on motorized sledges to rescue the three Flying Fortress crewmen still waiting on the ice. Only one hundred yards from the men, one of the sledges and its driver fell into a crevasse and disappeared. The other sledge tried to bring the three men back. One man was lost in a crevasse, and then the sledge broke down. The two men remaining from the bomber's crew and the lone rescuer had to winter over on the ice sheet—and these were not explorers equipped for this kind of thing. Five months later a plane finally reached the three men and lifted them safely off the ice.

The chain of airfields stretching across Greenland was built with more than ferrying and rescuing in mind. They were major stations of the CSR, the Crimson Staging Route, designed for casualties the Allies anticipated in the Normandy invasion of Europe. A hospital was set up at Narssarssuak for those too badly hurt to be sent on through the CSR.

None of this broke the isolation of the Greenlanders. The approximately two hundred and fifty Danes who administered the colony still enforced the century-old ban on ships entering the harbor for anything but unloading supplies. Many an American—and perhaps German—sailor must have looked longingly at land, particularly during the sudden and dangerous storms that can lash Greenland's seas, but he was not to feel it beneath his feet. The United States built its bases in relatively remote areas so that the Greenlanders would not be affected by military men or their material goods. Life went on for the Greenlanders as it had for two hundred years.

On May 8, 1945, almost a year after the Normandy invasion, the war in Europe ended. As a colony of Denmark, Greenland became a member in 1949 of the North Atlantic Treaty Organization—NATO—formed for the mutual defense of its members: Belgium, Canada, Denmark, France, Great Britain, Iceland, Italy, Luxembourg, the Netherlands, Norway, Portugal, and the United States. In 1951, Denmark agreed to lease certain areas in Greenland to the United States for a radar network for the DEW line and two air bases. The base at Sondre Stromfjord was to be shared with the Greenlanders as a commercial airport. And a base was built at the site of Freuchen and Rasmussen's trading post at Thule. A new town, Dundas, was built for the Polar Eskimos—also called the Thule Eskimos—to the north of Thule, so that they would not be exposed to the workmen and later the military men stationed there.

At Thule a radio antenna as tall as the Empire State Building was constructed, and radar equipment can detect a football-sized object three thousand miles away. In a little over ten seconds, Thule can tell the Strategic Air Command headquarters in Colorado Springs when and where a rocket is being fired in the northern half of the world, and where it will hit. The area around Thule was also designated for the burial of space waste, materials brought back from space but no longer usable.

One hundred and twenty miles west of Thule lie the remains of one of the most fascinating cities in the world, Camp Century. Built into the ice sheet in 1960 and closed five years later when its usefulness was over, it was the world's first atomic city, powered by a nuclear reactor and forty-two pounds of uranium. Camp Century had a main street connected to twenty-one tunnel streets, a chapel, and living quarters for one hundred to one hundred and fifty men. The reactor kept the outside ice frozen and the inside of the city warm—sometimes too warm, even in −40° C. weather. Actually, it was worse on a warm summer day when a door opened to the outside let in only warm air. Strangely enough, overheated buildings are a common problem in Greenland, where eveybody seems to keep the heat up to tropical levels.

Some of the work at Camp Century was a military secret, as it is in Thule. Much of the work was scientific; a great amount of research was done on the nature of the ice sheet, on living and working in the Arctic and using the materials at hand—namely ice and snow—to build. Researchers examined the snow that fell on the earth when dinosaurs were alive, when the Caesars ruled, when Christ was born, when the Norsemen first came to Greenland. And from what was learned it became possible to predict what the climate of the world would be in future centuries.

And still the Greenlanders lived as they had for two hundred years.

But now the bases were bringing in many more scientists, along with engineers, workers, their wives and families, mostly Danish, and a lot of goods, mostly American. You cannot stop an entire people from looking about them. The Greenlanders could see, and they were made curious by what they saw. So they looked again, and wanted what they saw. And they needed some of it—their living conditions were primitive and shockingly harsh by the standards of most of the world.

7

Today—and Tomorrow

A hunter who must use a bow and arrow or a spear when he knows about guns will not be satisfied until he acquires guns to better provide for his people. When he has the guns he will need bullets. If he cannot make bullets and guns himself, he will be dependent on those who can. A woman who must chew the hide of a seal to soften it for clothing will look longingly at the cheapest ready-made cloth and value it more than her magnificent furs. So what if it doesn't keep out the cold as well? She will have ready-made cloth, then a sewing machine, then ready-made dresses. And she may not chew the hide of the seal again, but instead will become dependent on those who can sew cloth into dresses.

The Danes tried to prevent this spiral, to keep their ways and American ways from influencing the Greenlanders' culture. The Danish hands-off policy was applauded by those who deplored the intrusion of foreign elements in the cultures of the United States and Canadian Eskimos. But the Danes did bring in economic, social, and political controls, and made the Greenlanders dependent on their paternalism—their missionaries, their coffee, tea, sugar, and tobacco—and their protection. And change cannot be denied, good or bad, for stagnation is always worse. In a world where the surgeon's scalpel can cure, why should a Greenlander die of appendicitis? A Greenlander's lifespan was only *thirty-two* years in the 1950s when scientists were getting ready to build the world's first atomic city in Greenland and could eavesdrop on missiles thousands of miles away. Disease, particularly tuberculosis, devastated the population. Hunger is never attractive, no matter how many generations have become accustomed to it. Rotten meat is not nutritious. Urine is not healthy to wash in. Drafty shacks are not necessarily historic

East Greenland home, 1930s.

Children like these were doomed to an early death until the 1950s, when Greenland entered the modern world.

Greenlandic women wore their hair tightly drawn back and bound with
a colored ribbon, which showed their marital status: blue for married,
red for unmarried. Most went bald at an early age because the hair
was pulled so tight. They are now discouraged from doing this.

dwellings to be cherished. No matter how protective of Greenland's culture the Danes wanted to be, they did not want to keep the Greenlanders from the benefits they could reap from the growth of knowledge in the world.

When Denmark had time to come to her feet after World War II, she looked at the Greenlanders' poverty and decided to end the island's isolation and bring its people into the modern world. The Royal Greenland Commission energetically took on the task and poured money into the country. Homes, hospitals, and schools went up, one after another. Construction centered around towns—4,500 housing units were rapidly built in only eighteen villages. Population was drawn in from outlying villages—as in Hans Egede's time, and for the same reasons: to make administration easier and to accomplish change more rapidly.

The pace was *too* fast. Faced with five-story cement apartment houses stretching for blocks, central heating, indoor plumbing, and the automobile all within a few years, the Greenlanders were overwhelmed. The Danes, too, were having trouble adjusting to Greenland. Houses built in the town of Narssaq blew away because the Danish builders had not listened to Greenlanders' warnings about particularly bad wind conditions there. In Holsteinborg, the permafrost proved not so permanent when new buildings caused the permafrost to melt and their foundations caved in.

When those and similar construction problems were finally solved, and the Greenlanders were able to move into their new low-rent housing, there were cultural problems. They had no furniture. And they didn't have any idea at all how to live in apartments. What to do with bathtubs? They used them for cutting up and storing seals. What to do with garbage? They were accustomed simply to tossing it into a corner or out into the snow or to the dogs. And how to live among strangers? Once they had shared; now they were concerned with what's mine and what's yours, and with theft. Once the best hunter was the most esteemed member of the community; now who would be?

Diets changed. Wild meat has twice the protein and far less fat than meat from the store, but when Greenlandic children began to eat beef regularly, seal and whale proved too rich for them to digest easily. The milk and milk products sent to Greenland from the many dairy farms that make Denmark rich made Greenlanders sick. Some Inuit, like some Jews, certain Mediterranean groups, and various other people around the world, lack the enzymes necessary for the digestion of milk. Beer, potato chips, and sugar products hit the Greenlanders all at once. Suddenly there were problems with high blood pressure, heart disease, gallstones, and bad teeth—so many bad teeth that dental care for children was made compulsory. In 1982, there was still a one-year wait for a dentist's appointment in Godthaab.

Now the Greenlanders had to handle money, decide on careers, plan for the future. And the future was limited, for there was little industry in Greenland.

Families once dependent on one another for survival—for hunting and preparing skins and sewing clothes and sharing joys and sorrows—began breaking up. Alcohol took loneliness and fear away, and alcohol consumption zoomed higher in Greenland than anywhere else in the world. In 1979, alcohol rationing began, but so did a black market and a heavy trade in ration coupons. Venereal diseases became epidemic.

Despite all the money the Danes poured into Greenland, or perhaps because of the money, the Greenlanders felt hopeless. The suicide rate became gigantic, particularly among young men. Lack of occupation, lack of opportunity, lack of familiarity with the world and the resulting feelings of inferiority in dealing with it . . . no one can be really sure of all the reasons for the despair.

To many it seemed as though the Greenlanders would fare better

Tasty eating.

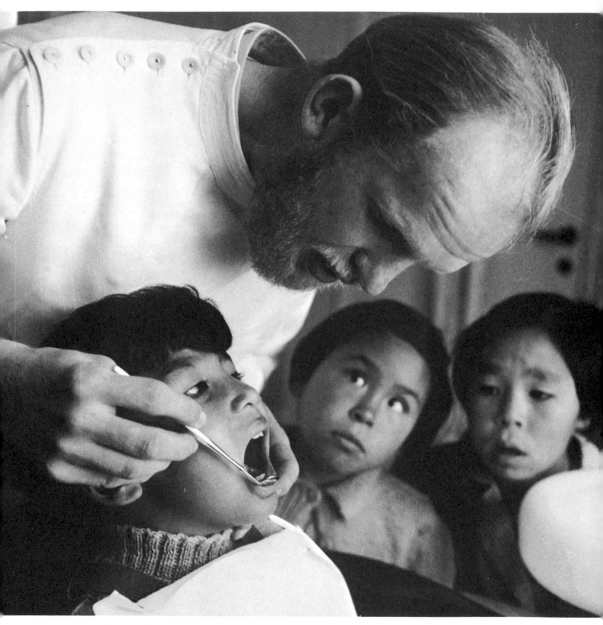

Open wide.

if they had more control over what happened to them, in particular more political control. In 1953 Greenland was given equal status with Denmark, and two members from Greenland were sent to the Folketing, the Danish parliament. A country-wide Provincial Council replaced small regional councils and handled matters of purely Greenlandic concern. But, of course, the Folketing remained in control, and the Folketing was mainly Danish.

In 1978, the Provincial Council proposed a scheme for self-government, or home rule, in Greenland. That autumn the Folketing set up the legislation, and the Greenlanders voted for self-government on January 17, 1979. Greenland became *Talâdlit-Nunât*, Land of the People. Talâdlit is the Greenlandic equivalent of Inuit—they both mean "The People." Greenlandic replaced Danish as the official language, and the Greenlanders now control all their internal affairs.

The Greenlandic governing body is the *Landsting*, a kind of Congress with between eighteen and twenty-one popularly elected representatives. A *Landsstyre* of three to five members acts as the executive body and is headed by the leader of the majority party, who has come to be called the premier. But Denmark still supports Greenland.

Greenland retains control over her mineral resources, like cryolite and coal, but plans for their development can still be vetoed in Denmark. Any monies received for minerals must also first go to Denmark to repay her for the support she gives the Greenlanders. Anything left will be shared between the two. Greenland and Denmark may be made rich some day by Greenland's minerals. Cryolite is giving out, but northern Greenland contains lead, copper, tin, and zinc. East Greenland has molybdenum, used for making steel, and chromite, zinc, and iron. Coal, regaining importance as an alternative energy source, has been mined in Greenland and exported since 1770. And there are an estimated four thousand tons of uranium near Narssaq. The minerals under the ice sheet are probably fabulous, but they are unobtainable with today's technology. Yet who knows what tomorrow will bring? Ten years ago the idea of ships drilling for oil in the ice-cluttered Davis Strait was unthinkable, but today there are three rigs out there during the summer months. Icebergs that drift too close for comfort simply get towed out of the way.

Oil and minerals may make Greenland very rich someday, but not right now. For now, fish are her main source of income. The prawns of Greenland's Disko Bay are said to be the best in the world, and shrimping is a promising export industry. Once fishing was considered a fit occupation only for women and for men unable to hunt. Today it is the men who fish. If they have to, they work alongside the women in the fish processing factories. But many of the men will not do this while the fishing season is on, even when they have caught all the fish government quotas allow. Sometimes there are not enough people to process the catch, and then it rots.

Cod, once the basis of the fishing industry, are decreasing because of a slight change in the temperature of the waters off Greenland. Salmon is now the main catch, but other countries are complaining that the salmon the Greenlanders sell are coming from *their* rivers. So Denmark has imposed a quota on the catch—infuriating the Greenlanders. It was over the issue of fishing rights that Greenlanders voted to pull their country out of the European Economic Community, the Common Market, to which they had belonged as a part of Denmark. Greenland wants no quotas. She wants exclusive fishing rights up to one hundred miles off her coast, and she sees no profit in making concessions to other countries, despite receiving $20 million a year from the Common Market, and having been supported for hundreds of years by Denmark.

A small industry in sheepfarming exists in the south of Greenland where there is still grazing land of the sort found by Eric the Red. Greenland also has an ice cube industry: ice cubes from Greenland's icebergs are exported in a very limited amount. They are special in-

The Provisional Council in session.

Village in southern Greenland. Note the sheep at left.

[106]

deed, for they are made of glacial ice millions and millions of years old. They are full of air bubbles that explode when the cubes are dropped into a drink.

Greenland is hoping to develop tourism as an industry, because tourists bring a lot of money into a country to buy food, lodging, souvenirs, and clothing. But tourists must be very well-to-do to travel in Greenland. There are no roads connecting towns, so to get anywhere people must go by helicopter, airplane, dog sledge (only for the hardy), or in summer by boat along the western coast. Passenger voyages are forbidden in winter ever since the pride of Denmark's Arctic fleet, the *Hans Hedtoft,* hit an iceberg on her maiden voyage and sank on January 30, 1959, with all lives lost. Air passage between towns is expensive, and so are the layovers when frequent fogs set in and flights can't get out. Delays of several days are common; a week or two is not unheard of. Even by plane, it isn't easy to get around. To fly from Scoresbysund in the northeast to Godthaab on the west coast means flying to Iceland, then from Iceland to Denmark, from Denmark to Sondre Stromfjord, and finally from Sondre Stromfjord to Godthaab. Since planes don't fly every day, it may take two or three weeks to make the trip.

But the tourist will find a country that captures the imagination and the affections. The mountains, the midnight sun, the aurora borealis—northern lights—that flash in sheets of color through the sky and mind, the moon that seems to be a foot away and made of butter and never sets in winter, the green dawns, the deep blue fjords, the dry snow that makes a delicious crunching sound underfoot—these are powerful attractions. So is the sense of human courage, of endless time, of a meaning beyond the present.

The cold is not as great a problem as one might think, so long as the weather is dry and windless, and the tourist is properly dressed. Indeed, heat is more of a problem, since interiors are often kept at uncomfortably high temperatures.

This Coast Guard C130 is "plugged in" so its fuel won't freeze.

The towns are crowded and small, built around the original colonies. Tiny wooden houses are painted gay blues, reds, and yellows. New concrete apartment houses stretch row upon row and appear sadly out of place. Wood seems to suit Greenland better than concrete.

The hills on which the towns are perched are mounted by wooden stairways connected to wooden walkways. Pipes supported by wooden blocks carry cables for power. Parked vehicles—including airplanes—are kept plugged into outlets so their fuel won't freeze.

Pipes carrying water and sewage must be heated and insulated or their contents will freeze and plug up the works. Utilidors, insulated wooden casings, enclose the pipes, and roads and stairways climb over them. It costs tens of thousands of dollars to connect one house to these pipelines. So water is usually bought from someone who goes out to an iceberg and collects pieces of ice for melting. Ice close to home is suspect, especially where there are dogs about, and "Don't eat the yellow ice" is a time-honored warning all over the Arctic. The lack of water also makes firefighting a terrible problem.

Sewage is collected in "honey bags," plastic bags lining a pail. The bags are put outside to freeze, and the honey truck collects them and replaces them with empty ones. Some communities have incinerators to burn sewage and garbage, or ramps built over the sea on which the honey trucks pull up and then empty their bags—when the water isn't frozen.

Once, the Greenland dog was the waste disposal system. Greenland dogs are not pets. They are not allowed in southern Greenland at all, where they are not needed to pull sledges. Wild and mean—some say the dogs are more than half wolf—they eat everything in sight, including human waste. They have been known to eat one another, and people, too. Imagine having to go out in the darkness and beat off hungry dogs!

In Greenland, where the days of winter and the nights of summer may be a mere hour or two long, time and darkess take on different meanings. It's hard to keep a sense of time in Greenland, to get up to go to work or to school. Children have never been made to go to bed; forcing a child to do anything has never been the Eskimo—or Inuit—way. Getting to school on time has not been the Inuit way either; pupils were accustomed to wandering into class when they happened to get up. That, too, is changing in Greenland.

Every young person is educated, free, to the level he or she desires and can achieve. In the small outlying villages, catechists are still the only teachers. Only the large cities have high schools. Many high school students must therefore be boarded out. Greenland's system of schooling is better than that of any other country in the Arctic, and there are more schools per child than there are in Denmark. But most of the teachers in Greenland's schools are Danish and speak only Danish. Students have to conquer the Danish language before they can get on with their studies.

The training of Greenlandic teachers is the first priority in Greenland today. There are teacher training colleges in Greenland, but they are not on the level of those in Denmark or the United States.

Greenlandic high school. The dormitory is on the left.

Greenlandic classroom.

Father teaching son traditional kayaking skills.

There is one general college, but most students go to Denmark for higher education. Living in Denmark, away from home, family, and friends, is a difficult adjustment for most young Greenlanders, and many succumb to homesickness before they finish their educations.

But education by itself will not help the Greenlanders that much. Every year, some fifteen hundred jobs have to be found for those getting out of school—and there aren't that many jobs around when the population is barely fifty thousand. The unemployment rate in Greenland is about 35 percent. In the United States, there was great horror when the jobless rate reached 10 percent. At the same time, the literacy rate—the percentage of people who can read and write—is 100 percent in Greenland and has been since the end of the nineteenth century. In the United States today well over ten million people cannot read and write. One hundred percent literacy is a remarkable achievement, and Greenland has a body of literature of its own of over one thousand titles.

In the schools the Danes encourage the teaching of traditional skills, like kayak-building, so that the Greenlanders will be proud of their heritage. But young people show little interest in learning these skills when readymade goods and services are available to them. Why learn to build a snow igloo or to live off the land when the igloo will never be used and the supermarket is down the street? But the supermarkets are still dependent on Danish money and on Danes to run them. Only recently have Greenlanders had the desire and the ability to accumulate money and obtain government permission to open up small stores and businesses of their own. And only recently have the Greenlanders recognized the absolute necessity of developing work opportunities for themselves.

The Greenlanders must reject Danish paternalism in order to grow, yet Greenland needs the two and a half million dollars the Danes spend annually to support them. Until Greenlandic industries, businesses, and professions develop to the point where the Greenlanders can sustain themselves, they will be dependent on the Danes. Their only hope for independence lies with education: educating the educators, the doctors, the dentists, lawyers, architects, administrators, clerks, bookkeepers, secretaries, accountants ... the people Greenland must have in order to run their own country.

Greenland's entry into the modern world has been painful and imperfect, and that is why there is so much alcoholism, depression, and suicide. But many good things have happened, too. Tuberculosis has been wiped out; housing, though ugly, is infinitely better than before, and healthier. Small, inexpensive, do-it-yourself houses are supplementing the huge concrete complexes. The houses are bought on mortgages with low interest rates and give the owners the pride of workmanship as well as ownership. Life expectancy is twice what it once was—it is now sixty-five years and climbing. Infant mortality has declined, and the birthrate is so much higher that controlling measures are being encouraged.

The Greenlanders are still hunters. Hunting for anything other than essential food is frowned upon by many people today, but not by most Greenlanders, or by most Inuit, for that matter. Killing seals to make fur coats may seem absurd and wasteful to some, but the Inuit around the world see it as a way to make the money they so badly need. The campaign to stop the wearing of furs causes the Inuit anger and fear, because it threatens their livelihood. And stopping the hunting of whales, a primary concern of many wildlife conservationists, seems almost sacrilegious to the Inuit. They say it is their time-honored right, it is in their blood, to kill the whale. The hue and cry of alien cultures against the cultural values of the Inuit is making the Greenlander furious.

Denmark recognizes the Greenlanders' dilemma, as well as the need to conserve wildlife. They ask, and the Greenland government agrees, that catches be limited and that the traditional kayak and

A blend of old and new.

Skinning a seal. This is usually the woman's job. This one bends
at the waist in typical Greenlandic fashion.

harpoon be used rather than modern weapons and transportation.
Many Greenlanders comply, but others use explosive heads on their
harpoons or charter a plane to go north and shoot musk oxen or
reindeer, or pretend to hunt the walrus for food but in fact take its
ivory tusks and leave the carcasses to rot. And the *right* to hunt or
fish to capacity, whether one actually does it or not, is the sticking
point for most Greenlanders.

Hard hunting.

Understanding different cultures, different values, has never been easy. The Greenlanders and other Inuit are on a collision course with the environmentalists of the United States and Canada in particular. Most people assume that those who live close to the land are concerned with the preservation of all animal life. They tend to believe that primitive peoples killed only what they could eat. This is not so. On the contrary, hunting societies often killed all they could, ate what they could, and threw away the rest. For Greenlanders, preserving food for tomorrow was a concept that came in with electricity and refrigerators. Even though the Arctic seems to be one big deep freeze, the Eskimos couldn't have stored food outside—it would have frozen too deeply for blubber lamps to defrost quickly, or it would have been rapidly eaten by dogs and other animals. So the Eskimos learned to eat all the fresh meat they could, while they could, and then they ate rotten meat—and enjoyed that, too.

Hunting was hard, so that if it was possible to kill, the hunter had no qualms about overkilling, or about a species running out. The Greenlanders revered the souls of the animals they killed, sprinkling water on the mouth of a newly dead seal, for instance, to placate its spirit and insure further good hunting. But they killed when they could and all they could, and were glad for it.

Greenlanders are not insensitive to other ecological issues either. Some are even strident, demanding the United States pay Greenland for polluting its air with planes. The Greenlanders themselves fly everywhere, so the objection to American planes seems to be based less on clean air and more on the possibility of getting money. Other ecological issues are perhaps more important ones: the need for using ecologically sound techniques in developing resources from mining and oil drilling in the Davis Strait, for instance. Issues such as these were discussed at a landmark Inuit Circumpolar Conference held in June, 1977, to which Greenland sent eighteen delegates and hundreds of observers. The conference aired many other problems of the Arctic dweller, such as the inadequacy of transportation within countries and from one Arctic land to another, and the importance of local control of wildlife, not control by American or European environmental pressure groups.

Greenland has political control of her destiny. But the Danish people and Danish money still support Greenland. If Greenland wants an Inuit identity rather than a Danish one, vision and courage, education and wisdom, are needed to bring her to her rightful place in the world community of the twenty-first century.

Bibliography

A book such as this can only touch the peaks of Greenland's story. For further reading, here are the books used in researching *Greenland: Island at the Top of the World*. Many are rare though sometimes found in libraries and old book stores. They are well worth pursuing.

The Arctic World. London: T. Nelson & Sons, 1876.

Babock, William H. *Legendary Islands of the Atlantic*. New York: American Geographical Society, 1922.

Carstensen, A. Riis. *Two Summers in Greenland*. London: Chapman and Hall Limited, 1890.

Commission for the Direction of the Geological and Geographical Investigations in Greenland. *Greenland*. 3 vols. Copenhagen: C. A. Reitzel; London: Humphrey Milford Oxford University Press, 1928.

Crantz, David. *History of Greenland*. London: Printed for the Brethren's Society for the furtherance of the Gospel among the Heathens, 1767.

Dash, Paul R. *The Cook-Ed-Up Peary-Odd-Ical Dictionary and Who's Hoot*. Boston: John W. Luce and Company, 1910.

deLaguna, Frederica. *Voyage to Greenland*. New York: W. W. Norton & Company, Inc., 1977.

Du Chaillu, Paul. *The Land of the Long Night*. New York: Charles Scribner's Sons, 1914.

Dyson, James. *The World of Ice*. New York, Alfred A. Knopf, 1972.

Dyson, John. *The Hot Arctic*. Boston & Toronto: Little, Brown and Company, 1979.

Freuchen, Peter. *Arctic Adventure*. New York: Farrar & Rinehart, 1935.

————. *Peter Freuchen's Book of the Eskimos*. Cleveland: The World Publishing Company, 1961.

————, with David Loth. *Peter Freuchen's Book of the Seven Seas*. New York: Simon and Schuster, 1957.

————. *Vagrant Viking: My Life and Adventures*. Translated by John Hambro. New York: Julian Messner, Inc., 1953.

Fristrup, Borge. *The Greenland Ice Cap*. Washington: University of Washington Press, 1967.

Greely, Adolphus W. *A Handbook of Polar Discoveries*. Boston: Little, Brown, and Company, 1895.

————. *Report of the Proceedings of the United States Expedition to Lady Franklin Bay Grinnell Land*. 2 vols. Washington: Government Printing Office, 1888.

Hall, Charles Francis. *Life with the Esquimaux*. London: Sampson Low Son, Marston, 1865.

Hayes, Isaac I. *The Land of Desolation*. New York: Harper & Brothers, 1872.

Jones, Gwyn. *A History of theVikings.* London: Oxford University Press, 1968.

Kane, Elisha Kent. *Arctic Explorations in the Years 1853, 1854, 1855.* 2 vols. Philadelphia: Childs and Peterson, 1856.

Keely, Robert N. *In Arctic Seas.* Philadelphia: Rufus C. Hartranft, 1892.

Kent, Rockwell. *Rockwell Kent's Greenland Book or Salamina.* New York: Harcourt, Brace and Company, 1931.

————. *North by East.* New York: Brewer & Warren, 1930.

Malaurie, Jean. *The Last Kings of Thule.* Translated by Adrienne Foulke. New York: Dutton, 1982.

Matsch, Charles L. *North America and the Great Ice Age.* New York: McGraw Hill Book Company, 1975.

May, Charles Paul. *Animals of the Far North.* London: Abelard Schuman, 1964.

Nansen, Fridtjof. *Farthest North.* 2 vols. London: George Newnes, 1898.

————. *First Crossing of Greenland.* London: Longmans, Green and Company, 1898.

Nordenskjold, Otto, and Mecking, Ludwig. *Geography of the Polar Regions.* American Geographical Society, 1928.

Owen, Ruth Bryan. *Leaves from a Greenland Diary.* New York: Dodd, Mead & Company, 1937.

Oxenstierna, Eric. *The World of the Norsemen.* Cleveland: World Publishing, 1967.

Papanin, Ivan. *Life on an Ice Floe: Diary of Ivan Papanin.* Translated from the Russian. New York: Julian Messner, Inc., 1939.

Proctor, Everitt. *Men Against the Ice.* Philadelphia: Westminster Press, 1946.

Putnam, David Binney. *David Goes to Greenland.* New York: G. P. Putnam's Sons, 1926.

Sturluson, Snorri. *Heimskringla—the Olaf Sagas.* Vol. 1, "The Tale of the Greenlanders." Translated by Samuel Laing. New York: Everyman's Library, Dutton, 1914.

Scott, J. M. *Icebound.* London: Gordon & Cremonisi, 1977.

Stables, Dr. Gordon. *To Greenland and the Pole.* New York: A. L. Burt.

Stefansson, Vilhjalmur. *Greenland.* New York: Doubleday, Doran & Company, Inc., 1942.

————. *The Northward Course of Empire.* New York: The Macmillan Co., 1924.

Whitney, Caspar; Grinnell, George Bird; Wister, Owen. *Musk-Ox, Bison, Sheep & Goats.* New York: The Macmillan Co., 1904.

Wright, Helen S. *The Great White North.* New York: The Macmillan Co., 1910.

Pamphlet publications of the Ministry of Foreign Affairs of Denmark.

Index

PHOTOCREDITS

Photographs courtesy of: Danish Consulate at New York: pp. 55, 60, 97, 102, 105, 106, 110, 111, 112, 115, 116, 117, 174; The Explorers Club: pp. 79, 83; National Maritime Museum, Greenwich, England: p. 47; New York Public Library: p. 96; United States Coast Guard: pp. 13, 14, 16, 17, 18, 21, 35, 88, 91, 108.